Have you ever wondered why you are wired the way you are when it comes to your finances? Why can't you save? Why do you spend so much? Why are you so fearful of anything financially related? Why do you give so much that it truly hurts your bank account? Why are you so miserly? It is in seeking to understand the why that you can change for the better. This book will help you deeply examine your God-given money type. Once you understand your type you can find financial peace.

MICHELLE SINGLETARY, author of *The 21-Day Financial Fast* and personal finance columnist for *The Washington Post*

The Seven Money Types is not a book on how to manage money. Rather, it is a unique approach to understanding how you innately relate to handling money. You will likely find yourself in one of these seven types. It reveals the benefits and pitfalls of each type. A careful reading will help you make the most of who you are and better understand others who are wired differently. A fascinating concept.

GARY CHAPMAN, PhD, author, *The Five Love Languages*

To know Tommy Brown is to know a man of wisdom and courage. His wisdom is evident on every page of this book; his courage is reflected in his eagerness to truly live the words of the ancient sage who taught, "Who is wise? He who learns from everyone." Many books offer little or nothing. Other books are moving and heartwarming. But this book by Tommy Brown is in a rare category: it has the power to actually transform your life for the better. Be prepared: the road you are on will never be the same after reading (and studying) this down-to-earth spiritual masterpiece.

RABBI ARTHUR KURZWEIL, teacher and author

Tommy Brown's financial insight and passion for teaching others about financial stewardship is undeniable! In his book *The Seven Money Types*, he teaches financial wellness strategies, but more than that, he teaches us how to understand the heart, or good intentions, behind our and our loved ones' financial decisions. This is *the* money book I recommend to my counseling clients!

SHANNON WARDEN, PhD, coauthor with Dr. Gary Chapman
of *Things I Wish I'd Known Before We Became Parents*;
assistant teaching professor, Wake Forest University

With compassion, Scriptural insights and pertinent examples from his pastoral and professional experience, Tommy Brown makes the convincing case that to align the ways we think and feel about money with how God designed us leads to empowerment—to do good in the world and nurture relationships, including with those who, by God's design, may view money differently. He teaches us to be gentle with ourselves and reminds us that financial well-being is not based on the amount of money we have in the bank but on the "why" that drives our decisions, hopes, dreams, and partnerships.

MARIA HENSON, Pulitzer Prize Winner

Using seven biblical money types as examples of financial stewardship, Tommy Brown presents a most creative teaching on the ways each of us can use well the money we are entrusted with. You will enjoy and be stimulated by this book!

DR. GEORGE O. WOOD, General Superintendent
of the Assemblies of God

The Seven Money Types does for finances what Gary Chapman's *The Five Love Languages* does for personal relationships. If you want a greater sense of clarity surrounding why you relate to money the way you do, look no further than this book. Not only will *The Seven Money Types* give you a greater sense of self-understanding, it will also give you a deeper appreciation for the unique way God has wired each one of us. Reading this book and realizing I am a "Jacob type" has changed everything for me, financially speaking. I encourage you to read this book. You won't be sorry you did.

REV. AUSTIN CARTY, *Survivor* cast member; author,
High Points and Lows

Tommy Brown's *The Seven Money Types* is an insightful analysis of how people respond to money and wealth. I have read many books on the topic, and I manage money professionally. Brown's discovery of the wealth attributes of key biblical figures and the related *shadow sides* should appeal to sophisticated asset managers and individual savers alike. It is definitely worth reading.

JAY HELVEY, partner, Cassia Capital Partners LLC

A fresh, liberating perspective on how Christians can think about faith and finances. Moving beyond tired dichotomies, Brown points us toward a healthy relationship with money and possessions. I highly recommend *The Seven Money Types*.

FRED BAHNSON, author, *Soil and Sacrament*; faculty,
Wake Forest University

Through a creative use of biblical archetypes, Brown helps us to see that our relationship to money is about more than spending and saving. Our relationship to money mirrors our relationships with God and with one another. This book offers practical suggestions, but more than that, opens the reader to understand how handling money is a spiritual practice.

GAIL R. O'DAY, Dean and Professor of New Testament and Preaching,
Wake Forest University School of Divinity

Tommy Brown has given us a unique perspective on how God has shaped us to steward resources. As you study the journeys of these seven biblical characters, your own financial path will become clearer.

LEIGHTON FORD, president, Leighton Ford Ministries

Tommy is a personal friend and one of the most knowledgeable persons I know in his field of expertise. Everyone who reads this book will gain great personal benefit.

DAVID COOPER, senior pastor, Mount Paran Church of God

The
SEVEN MONEY TYPES

DISCOVER HOW GOD WIRED
YOU TO HANDLE MONEY

TOMMY BROWN

ZONDERVAN

The Seven Money Types
Copyright © 2017 by Thomas Brown

Requests for information should be addressed to:
Zondervan, *3900 Sparks Dr. SE, Grand Rapids, Michigan 49546*

Library of Congress Cataloging-in-Publication Data

Names: Brown, Tommy, 1979- author.
Title: The seven money types : discover how God wired you to handle money / Tommy
Brown.
Other titles: 7 money types
Description: Grand Rapids, Michigan : Zondervan, [2017] | Includes bibliographical
references.
Identifiers: LCCN 2016039064 | ISBN 9780310335443 (softcover)
Subjects: LCSH: Finance, Personal--Religious aspects--Christianity. | Money--Religious
aspects--Christianity.
Classification: LCC HG179 .B7476 2017 | DDC 332.024--dc23 LC record available at
https://lccn.loc.gov/2016039064

The stories and anecdotes in this book are based on true experiences, but some are compilations.
In others the identifying details have been changed to protect the person's privacy.

This book is intended to provide general information and assumes no liability for its
effectiveness. In all cases, seek the advice of a certified financial planner.

The author is donating a portion of this book's proceeds to support educational organizations
that enhance and strengthen Jewish and Christian relationships.

Published in association with the literary agency of Wendy Sherman Associates, Inc.

Art direction: Curt Diepenhorst
Interior design: Denise Froehlich

First printing January 2017 / Printed in the United States of America

This book is dedicated to my wife, Elizabeth,
and our children, Seri and Seth,
who embody the best and most beautiful
of all I hope for and hold dear.

CONTENTS

ACKNOWLEDGMENTS

Rabbi Arthur Kurzweil opened my eyes to the truth. He's a trusted friend, and as a Christian, I'm honored and humbled that he lets this Gentile call him *rabbi*. I've also learned why Saint Paul encouraged the branches not to forget the root as I've drawn such strength, wisdom, and love from this man's friendship, scholarship, and religious tradition. If not for him, this book would not have been written.

Fred Bahnson journeyed with me through the early stages of this manuscript and believed in this concept. His input and support were invaluable.

Austin Carty was the first to breathe life into the idea of writing a book about money types. I drew the concept for him on the back of a napkin mid-flight between North Carolina and Connecticut. In five words—"I think that's a book"—he ignited a passion inside me. More than that, he's walked with me each step of the journey. He, too, is a trusted friend.

Chris, Gileah, and the rest of the Taylor family have loved and supported my family in ways that constantly remind me there is nothing better than good friends. Chris has remained a steady companion through both life's joys and fears.

Wendy Sherman, my literary agent, provided continual support and encouragement, advocating for this book and helping shape its direction.

Carolyn McCready, my editor, drew out of this manuscript its best and brightest potential. I'm inspired by her dedication, not just to her writers and the material, but to the readers she hopes to serve through her work in shaping content.

Without the marketing support of Tom Dean, Keith Finnegan, and their incredible team at Zondervan, you wouldn't know this book exists.

My parents, Tom and Alisha Brown, are constant encouragers and willing readers of endless drafts.

Kevin Frack paid attention to my life in a way that helped me realize my deepest sense of call—my love for writing, teaching, and connecting the dots between faith and finances.

Hayes Henderson provided valuable creative dialogue and partnership.

Chris Lawson provided a platform for me to share my writings with others and helped me better serve my audience with content.

Rabbi Mark Strauss Cohn and Dr. Clinton Moyer helped me see in clearer view the many faces of the Hebrew Bible.

Sandra Graff instilled a love for the written word in me when I was a high school student. Her enthusiasm for literature made me love to read and write.

My brother, Christopher Brown, helped analyze this book's assessment results in a way that provided direction for the trajectory the instrument would take.

T. J. Shaffer offered wisdom and insight that helped me remain centered on the most important relationships and things in life while I wrote this book.

Mark MacDonald proved integral in my gaining clarity on

the role this book would play in helping people resolve financial tensions. He's the best I've met at helping churches and individuals dial in to their unique mission and calling.

Elaine Tooley provided editing and insights for this book's proposal.

Brett and Stephanie Eaton offered encouragement, support, and feedback on the manuscript in its earliest and most formative stages.

Allen Vesterfelt performed layout and design for this book's proposal.

Dr. Shannon Warden's wisdom, insight, and expertise proved vital in developing the assessments.

Dr. Gary Chapman's belief in and support of this material are deeply appreciated. I cherish the insights I've gained from his decades of ministry and writing.

Rich Wall and Matt Canter played a unique role in this book. They helped me devise creative ways to work a full-time job, be a father and husband, and create space to research this material in a financially responsible way.

Dr. Mike and Darla Rakes encouraged me, as a minister, to keep noticing and communicating the myriad connections between God and money.

To my friends and colleagues at Wake Forest University, thank you for your support of this project and for embodying the deep and true spirit of *Pro Humanitate*.

The following people walked with me for two months as readers, dialogue partners, and supporters as we explored this book together. Their feedback and encouragement helped tailor the book in important ways: Kristen Edgar, Joseph Bullin, Cassie Pruitt, Dr. Matt and Michelle Ravish, Nathaniel and Meredith Branscome, Kent and Bonnie Gravely, and Ashley and Felix Reyes.

INTRODUCTION

We long for financial well-being—the ability to handle resources in a way that's true to our deepest sense of self while maintaining healthy financial thoughts, emotions, and attitudes. This experience of financial well-being is possible if we understand how God designed us in one of seven ways to handle money. I call these ways the seven money types.

Financial well-being transcends earning a large paycheck or being able to balance our budget and afford desired purchases. We know this because regardless of how much money flows through our hands, we often experience financial tensions, fears, and anxiety brewing beneath the surface. These tensions are complex and manifest in every sphere of our lives—relational, professional, physical, spiritual, and emotional.

If we're seeking authentic financial well-being, we'll have to look within ourselves; we'll need to look to God. We must do more than balance our budgets, increase our savings accounts, and invest for the future. We'll need to cease striving for what we do not have and reach deeper into who we are. We'll need to increase our awareness of how and why we (and others) think, feel, and act the ways we do financially. Financial well-being is not based in amounts—how much or little we have—but rather in understanding and embracing how we relate to money. Otherwise, we can have immense wealth and never enjoy it.

I've experienced the power of understanding money types firsthand. I didn't develop these ideas in a laboratory or clinic; I'm not a scientist or psychologist. This concept emerged in real-time practice in my work as a pastor, scholar, and financial management educator who is continually learning more about the unique and endless ways God has designed us to relate to money. My goal is to help you partner with the work of the Spirit and the Scriptures to probe the depths of your inner relationship to money so you can experience financial well-being.

The Seven Money Types contains nothing new, although it's unlikely you've ever considered your relationship to money in the ways you're about to. In fact, this process is based on one of the oldest stories about human existence the Bible affords us: what happened in the garden of Eden. This story cuts right to the core of who we are. In the upcoming pages, we'll explore an ancient, scriptural pathway that leads us to resolve our deepest financial tensions, gives us clarity about why we relate to money the way we do, and positions us for greater intentionality and impact in the area of our finances.

How we intuitively relate to money tells us something about how God uniquely wired each of us. In other words, the times you struggle with money as well as the times you enjoy it, your emotions toward it, and when you wish your financial situation was different—all these signal what's deep inside you worth noticing and to what you should pay attention. Your money type is telling you something.

When your eyes are opened to the truths money types reveal, it will change how you relate to God and money. These simple yet profound lessons provide the insights needed to remain confident and at peace in any financial situation, to finally understand why you think, feel, and act the ways you do with money.

Let's begin so you can discover and grow in your unique, God-designed money type.

CHAPTER 1

THE SEVEN BIBLICAL MONEY TYPES

For the better part of a decade, I talked with friends, pastors, professors, and financial planners about my theory that God created every human being with a unique money type. That is, God designed each person in his image to relate to resources in general, and money in particular, in a distinct way. I took stabs at identifying what those money types were and, as a pastor seeking ways to convey these important truths to others, I extensively explored the Scriptures in search of the biblical characters who best represented the particular money types I saw in my everyday work in the area of faith and finances.

As I taught financial management courses, both at the congregational and collegiate levels, I dialed in to the unique ways people feel, think, and act concerning money. I noticed how often people felt guilty for not thinking the way someone else thought about money. I often heard phrases like "I'm just 'bad' with money." Conversely, I recognized how regularly some people felt superior because their way of relating to resources more closely resembled the prevailing culture's attitudes toward what was defined as *financial success*. They were "good" with money.

Interestingly, most people seemed to think there is only one—or maybe two—"right" way to handle money. But I believed there were more "right" ways to relate with money, and that it had everything to do with how God designed us. I began reading and studying about this topic in earnest.

Eventually my theological studies required that I take a course on Judaism, which transpired in Falls Village, Connecticut. There, unaware he is one of today's leading Jewish thinkers, I met Rabbi Arthur Kurzweil, and he became a dear friend and dialogue partner. Our hearts connected immediately, and within a few hours I shared my belief that God designed humans in his image and that the unique way each of us is designed in God's image affects how we handle money.

Rabbi Kurzweil listened and smiled. I didn't know whether his smile meant he thought I was a complete heretic and that he was about to destroy my theory or that I was in fact onto something. When I shared with him my thesis that biblical characters such as Abraham, Moses, and David served as money types who embody and clarify certain aspects of what it means to be made in God's image, he leaned in and whispered, "The characters you're looking for, they're already picked. They were selected long ago. You're not crazy." Now he had my full attention.

We talked late into the night. I learned not only that my intuitions and research were valid, but that for ages many people of Jewish faith have held as part of their faith tradition that distinct aspects of God's image are revealed through seven biblical characters: Abraham, Isaac, Jacob, Joseph, Moses, Aaron, and David. These individuals are so prominent and memorable within the

Scriptures because each of their lives represents something significant about what it means to be human, to be made in God's image. They represent what we aspire to attain.

Streams of the Jewish tradition affirm that, through their lives and stories, each of these individuals leads us into a clearer understanding of one aspect of what it means to be made in God's image. At this intersection their tradition merged with and informed my theory and experience in financial management and coaching. The seven biblical characters who represent seven aspects of God's image are the seven money types, because, as you'll soon discover, Scripture teaches that to be made in God's image is to properly steward creation and its resources, including money.

As a Christian, some of my views surrounding these traditions are certainly different from those of the Jewish tradition; nevertheless, I was able to discern areas of commonality and truth in this Jewish construct that enlightened my approach to clarifying and understanding the seven money types.

Over the following years, I studied the lives of these seven characters, selecting and drawing upon principles that aligned with my faith and experience in the Christian tradition. Viewing these seven biblical characters through the lens of money types affirmed my experience in pastoral ministry, financial coaching, and my biblical studies: people relate to the world around them (including how they relate to money) in seven primary ways, and these seven ways are modeled by these seven figures. Individually, each of the seven biblical figures inspires us to embrace the fullness of what it means to be made in God's image, especially in the ways we relate to money. When held together, they compose a breathtaking and inspiring picture of God's image—a life with God we've always dreamed of.

Now I've discovered the key to financial well-being is to cease striving for what you do not have and to reach deeper into who you are, into who God designed you to be, and to start your journey there. Then as you continually mature as a person of faith, your experience of how you handle money will deepen. And as you handle money differently, your faith experience will also deepen. Each makes an impact on the other because money matters are a primary space where we learn to trust God. God and money will begin to work together to give voice to your soul's longings as God uses your relationship to money to bring hope and healing into the world.

The Seven Money Types and God's Image

This journey to discovering your money type and experiencing financial well-being originates in a most familiar part of Jewish and Christian history. The ancient Jews safeguarded a story that reveals how God created humans as what we've come to call *imago Dei*, the image of God.

> Then God said, "Let us make humankind in our image, according to our likeness . . ." So God created humankind in his image, in the image of God he created them; male and female he created them. God blessed them, and God said to them, "Be fruitful and multiply, and fill the earth and subdue it; and have dominion over the fish of the sea and over the birds of the air and over every living thing that moves upon the earth." (Gen. 1:26–28 NRSV)

Astoundingly, humans are made in the image of God. The microcosm of human life reflects the macrocosm of divine reality; in other words, the smallness of our lives somehow depicts the bigness of God. This is mystery, and yet it is precisely where we must begin, from a biblical standpoint, if we hope to discover how we are designed to relate to the world around us, especially to money.

The assignment of God-imaged humans was to multiply and care for creation and its resources, which has come to include money. Forevermore, human fulfillment—a sense of peace and wholeness—would be wrapped up in how well we carried out this assignment. Thereby, the *imago Dei* would fill the whole earth, with God's love and light all over the place, all the time.

This image, however, was marred as our first parents transgressed God's ways by using resources (who can forget that forbidden apple?) in a manner incongruent with their souls' deepest desires—to know and love God forever. The way they handled resources affected their relationship with God. Since that time, God has worked to restore the *imago Dei* and make the world whole again, using humanity's relationship to resources to form faith in God and as an expression of God's love and care for the world. Jewish writer Leonard Fein thoughtfully expressed our challenge when he wrote, "We are called to see the beauty through the blemishes, to believe it can be restored, and to feel ourselves implicated in its restoration. We are called to be fixers."[1]

The story unfolds, and over the course of hundreds of years, God used seven individuals to shepherd his people and lead them back into his ways: Abraham, Isaac, Jacob, Joseph, Moses, Aaron, and David. Through their lives and teachings they carried a special message into the earth to remind humanity of what it's like to do life with God; indeed, what it's like to be made in God's image. Each of these seven characters revealed one of the seven aspects of what it means to be made in God's image. They guided God's people into their future, which was really a restoration of the best of their past, of what was lost in Eden.

Individually, each one highlights a unique aspect of what it means to be God-imaged:

Abraham offers God's hospitality.
Isaac demonstrates God's discipline.
Jacob reflects God's beauty.
Joseph depicts God's connection.
Moses manifests God's endurance.
Aaron embodies God's humility.
David influences with God's leadership.

While each of their lives demonstrated one aspect of God's image in a unique and clearly recognizable way, no single character fully embodied all aspects of God's image to the utmost degree. They all provided glimpses; none fully represented the totality of what it means to be made in God's image.

If the fullness of each of the seven aspects of God's image were realized, we'd behold the fullness of human potential. In both the Christian and Jewish traditions, this is realized in the personhood of the Messiah. Because none of us is perfect, each one of us is necessary to the human race to give us a clearer image of who God is and what life with God can be like. The apostle Paul put it like this:

Just as a body, though one, has many parts, but all its many parts form one body, so it is with Christ. For we were all baptized by one Spirit so as to form one body—whether Jews or Gentiles, slave or free—and we were all given the one Spirit to drink. Even so the body is not made up of one part but of many. Now if the foot should say, "Because I am not a hand, I do not belong to the body," it would not for that reason stop being part of the body. And if the ear should say, "Because I am not an eye, I do not belong to the body," it would not for that reason stop being part of the body. If the whole body were an eye, where would the sense of hearing be? If the whole body were an ear, where would the sense of smell be? But in fact God has placed the parts in the body, every one of them, just as he wanted them to be. If they were all one part, where would the body be? As it is, there are many parts, but one body. (1 Cor. 12:12–20)

We are not all Christians or Jews, but in a greater sense we are all part of a larger body of humanity. All of us—Christians, Jews, Buddhists, Muslims, and people of other faiths or no faith, such as atheists or agnostics—are made in God's image. Being made in God's image is not determined by confession or creed, but by God's own design and initiative.

We all reflect God's image in some way or another, and everyone has a money type. For the purposes of this book, however, I've focused the material toward a Judeo-Christian understanding of faith and finances, illustrating how understanding and embracing your money type helps you experience financial well-being and spiritual maturity in light of these beliefs and traditions.

The way we're designed in God's image affects how we relate to resources. Interestingly, when we explore scriptural stories about each of these seven shepherds, we'll notice that each shepherd relates to resources out of the aspect of divine image he represents. For example, Abraham represents hospitality, and we almost always see Abraham using his resources in hospitable ways. Isaac is different, approaching resources with an eye toward making the most out of whatever he has. He's a disciplined maximizer to the core. The same holds true of the other five biblical characters—each relates to resources out of the aspect of divine image he embodies. This makes perfect sense, from a scriptural perspective, because to be made in God's image is to care properly for resources and creation (Gen. 1:28).

The way each character related to resources flowed from the unique aspect of the image of God he represented. Therefore, for our purposes, they demonstrate the seven primary ways God's image is revealed in the earth through the way we handle resources.[2]

Revealing God's Image to the World

The Scriptures summon us into the story. Now we've received the invitation and commission to reveal God's image to the world, and to do so, we must discern and develop our relationship with money by discovering and growing in our money type. If we align the ways we think, feel, and act financially with how God designed us, we become his partners through our use of money to impact the world in profound ways.

Each of the seven biblical characters shows us some virtue we hope to attain; each represents something larger than life—something we emulate and something we know in our souls is a better and more holistic way of life. However, while we hope to grow in all aspects of what it means to be made in God's image, our souls typically gravitate toward one of seven pathways as it relates to God and money.

We're drawn to a certain character's story because it is, in some way, our story. It is as though our souls sing harmony to the melody of one of their stories. For example, perhaps you've always connected with David. Now you'll understand why.

Keep in mind that nobody is purely one type, and this is by design. Occasionally some people equally identify with more than one type. For example, you may find you equally identify with the Abraham and Aaron types.

All the types, to some degree or another, are at play in our lives. All the types are at work in our experience of the world and its resources, and we're meant to understand and grow in each of them. However, most often you'll resonate most strongly with one money type.

Other Factors That Affect Your Views of Money

God is not the only one who has shaped your thoughts and actions regarding money. The ways we relate to money are also shaped by our closest relationships. We've picked up practices and paradigms, or ways of thinking about the world, from these important connections.

While God uniquely shaped us to relate to creation and its resources, if we allow him to, he also works with the raw materials of our lives—both our genealogies and our most recent lived experiences—to form us into the best version of ourselves so we use money in the best ways possible. God's work interweaves the fabric of our stories. While we enter the world with certain dispositions and inclinations, our experiences along the way make an impact on and shape those inherent qualities.

As we begin this journey together, the most important step is the next step, and the next step is taken from the place where you now stand. You bring your full self into your next step, your deepest and most God-instilled inclinations and your past experiences. Really, there's no way or reason to neatly separate how God designed you from how life has shaped you—you are who you are, and God has been at work in it all.

Seeking to Understand *Why*

As we explore the various money types, keep in mind this important point: we're seeking to understand *why* we handle money the ways we do, which stem from our basic beliefs about money. For example, any money type can donate to a cause, but each of the types is motivated to do so for a particular reason. All types will make purchases, but understanding *why* each type approaches making a purchase for different reasons and understanding the emotions and thoughts they face is where we gain greater insights into how God has wired us. Essentially, we're paying attention to the thoughts and emotions that make an impact on how we handle money because this provides clues to how God has uniquely designed us. In the end, this understanding increases our sense of financial well-being.

Types and Their Shadow Sides

One more vital element must be understood if we want to experience financial well-being. Each type has what I call a shadow side. While the seven biblical characters provide us clearer images of what God is like and how life can be with God, they all had deep flaws that flowed from the shadow side of their lives. These flaws affected how they handled resources. For example, Isaac represents discipline, and the way he related to resources flowed out of a disciplined mindset—he sought to maximize whatever he had. His shadow side was fear, and because of this fear, he occasionally found himself concerned about how God would provide resources. When a shadow side of fear is coupled with a disciplined mindset, the potential for greed becomes very real. A disciplined pursuit of maximizing resources can morph into hoarding; fear turns disciplined inclinations into greed. Nevertheless, despite their shadow sides, God journeyed with them. So there is space for us to grow and develop as well.

A shadow side presents each of us with an opportunity to mature related to money. As you read about each of the seven types, you'll learn from his hang-ups and setbacks. Seeing the character's shadow side in action will help you become more aware of your own shadow side so you can guard against its tendencies.[3] The more we learn to recognize, understand, and even anticipate our own shadow sides the better positioned we are to keep them from affecting our otherwise healthy relationships with God and money. Each type's shadow side wrestles with the light of God's image seeking to shine forth; virtue and vice are in tension within and around each of them, and the same pertains to each of us. This is one reason we often have conflicting emotions internally and tensions with others externally related to money.

Because we're surrounded by unhealthy messages about money from the prevailing culture, and by faulty thinking, our shadow sides can become difficult to see. Perhaps our eyes have adjusted to the darkness to the point that we've become accustomed to it, not realizing there is an illuminated path just outside our awareness. I hope the Shadow Side section in the chapter about your money type will help you see your own shadow side with greater clarity.

Seeing God in Other Money Types

A person's money type influences the ways he or she thinks about, feels about, and acts with money. For this reason, it's vital that you glean insights on how to recognize other money types at work in those around you—both their strengths and shadow sides—so you can better relate to them.

Perhaps like me, you've been taught everyone should relate to money in certain ways. Rather than writing off someone's thoughts, emotions, or behavior as irrational, you can use the information in this book to help you consider how that person may be expressing—for better or worse—the uniqueness of God's image playing out through their money type, or perhaps how their shadow side is creating tension. While it may be enticing to read only about the type you perceive to be your own, it will be profitable to study each type, thereby preparing you to better understand your friends, relatives, and colleagues. Besides, you're meant to grow in all the types, maturing in your relationship to God and money. Each type is important to your spiritual and financial growth and development as a well-rounded person.

All the money types bring with them wonderful and challenging aspects. Understanding how a type is operating can bring great clarity to a situation, repairing relationships and allowing space for diverse ways of relating to money to emerge and work together. The degree to which we embrace and grow in our money types determines whether we are able to conquer our internal and relational financial tensions.

Beyond the Bottom Line

For so long we've been told we should relate to money in certain ways. We've instinctively known, however, that there's more to our relationship with God and money than just saving, spending, and giving, more than wealth or poverty. We are not that simple. We are diversely, divinely designed, and we can understand ourselves a little more clearly not by fitting into haphazard financial mantras or categories, but by looking more intently at God, his Word, and how we are made in his image informs the ways we—and others—relate to money.

Have you ever taken time to listen to your life, and to listen to God's voice in and through your life, to hear what he is saying to you about the way you are God-imaged? God-wired? Could the way you feel about and relate to money be part of God's design, and are you open to growing in your relationship to God and money as you embrace and mature in this God-design? Are you open to viewing money as a medium or tool through which you can give expression to your deepest, most God-centered passions?

The goal of this book is not to give practical advice on what to do with your money. You should seek a certified professional for assistance with learning how to give, save, spend, and invest your finances. I'm not a certified financial planner (though I've worked with them); I'm a student of the Scriptures with the heart of a pastor who, like you, believes life makes more sense in light of God and how he is revealed in the stories of Scripture. You will, however, learn much more about how you are wired financially. Hopefully, you'll emerge with more questions—and some helpful answers—while growing closer in your relationship with God and more at peace with your relationship to money.

Discover Your Money Type: The Seven Money Types Assessment

This assessment is designed to help you discern the way(s) you most clearly resonate with God's image related to finances. You're the expert on you, so view this assessment as a tool to point you in the right direction, but ultimately rely on what you know about yourself as you read the chapters. You'll sense when you discover your type.

Carefully consider the following statements. For each one, write a response in the space provided that most resembles how well you resonate with the statement. Try to answer the questions based on your most natural instincts, not how you've had to adapt given life circumstances. Also, don't fret over which response is the right response, how you *should* respond, or how you *wish* you could respond. You have been wonderfully designed, so there's no need to perform.

MONEY TYPES ASSESSMENT

RATING SCALE

0 = Rarely   1 = Sometimes   2 = Often   3 = Almost Always

ASSESSMENT

____ 1. I love budgeting.

____ 2. I regularly spend money to bless others and make them feel special.

____ 3. I focus on how to maximize my money.

____ 4. I plan to set up the next generation to win financially.

____ 5. Perhaps more than others, I enjoy spending money on meals or activities to get to know new people.

____ 6. When I see someone in financial need, I must do something about it.

____ 7. If I'm not careful, I spend more than I should giving gifts or hosting others.

____ 8. I am very organized with money.

____ 9. I use my resources to create beautiful environments or experiences.

____ 10. It drains my energy to make long-term financial plans.

____ 11. I spend more time thinking about what's possible financially than thinking about my present financial situation.

____ 12. When invited to a gathering, I love to contribute in a meaningful way.

____ 13. While I'm not wasteful, I do things first-class.

____ 14. I love sharing my dreams and plans for the future with others.

____ 15. I'm a tough negotiator who tries to get the best deal.

____ 16. When I see a person in need, I feel bad for having so many possessions.

____ 17. In my household or among friends, I'm viewed as the one with a good handle on how to deal with money.

____ 18. I have a clear view of my preferred financial future.

____ 19. I am financially frugal because it makes me feel secure.

____ 20. I'm engaged with many projects, groups, or charities in my community.

____ 21. I have a hard time accepting the generosity of others.

____ 22. When it comes to money, I keep the long-term in clear view.

____ 23. I enjoy motivating others to give money to projects.

____ 24. I intensely focus on items or experiences I desire.

____ 25. If I acquired $1,000 I didn't need, my strongest inclination would be to use it to pay off a debt or bill.

____ 26. I'm energized by imagining long-term financial possibilities for my personal life or company.

____ 27. I'm always looking for new ways to make money.

____ 28. I do just enough money management to function.

____ 29. I'm steady and consistent when it comes to the way I handle money.

____ 30. I enjoy partnering with others on projects or business ideas, even outside my regular job responsibilities.

____ 31. I have no problem spending money on myself.

____ 32. When it comes to money, I think, "You can't take it with you when you die."

____ 33. When making a purchase, I value getting what I want over getting the best deal.

____ 34. People view me as someone who can help them make an important connection with another person or group.

____ 35. I put my own desires last.

The seven money types are listed below. Write the score you gave yourself beside each question number. For example, if you scored 2 on question 7, write 2 in the space beside question 7 below, which is under the Abraham type. Then total your responses for each type.

SCORE

Abraham	Isaac	Jacob	Joseph
2. _____	3. _____	9. _____	5. _____
7. _____	15. _____	13. _____	14. _____
12. _____	19. _____	24. _____	20. _____
21. _____	25. _____	31. _____	30. _____
35. _____	27. _____	33. _____	34. _____
Total:_____	Total:_____	Total:_____	Total:_____

Moses	Aaron	David	
1. _____	6. _____	4. _____	
8. _____	10. _____	11. _____	
17. _____	16. _____	18. _____	
22. _____	28. _____	23. _____	
29. _____	32. _____	26. _____	
Total:_____	Total:_____	Total:_____	

The previous totals reflect the degree to which you resonate with each type. Now, transfer your totals to the chart below. This will provide a more complete picture of how you resonate with each of the seven money types.

Score	Type	Aspect of God's Image	Shadow Side
	Abraham	Hospitality	Self-sufficiency
	Isaac	Discipline	Fear
	Jacob	Beauty	Indulgence
	Joseph	Connection	Manipulation
	Moses	Endurance	Impatience
	Aaron	Humility	Instability
	David	Leadership	Selfishness

Your highest score in the chart above is your strongest money type. If you have more than one highest score, this indicates you strongly resonate with more than one type, which is entirely possible and absolutely normal. You're looking for your strongest inclinations, not necessarily a clear ranking. Also, become curious about your lowest scores. It is likely that these are the areas where you experience the greatest levels of internal and relational tension when it comes to money. Interestingly, the type with which we least resonate offers us the greatest potential for personal growth and internal balance. Remember, you're seeking not only to embrace your strongest money type, but to learn from and grow in other money types as well. Different types bring with them unique strengths, which will help you mature in areas you may desire to grow related to money.

Finally, it may be helpful to see your types ranked by the degree to which you resonate with each one. Below, list your results from greatest to least. If you have a tie, list them one after the other, in any order. You can revise this later if you sense one truly is stronger than the other.

Score	Type	Aspect of God's Image	Shadow Side

CHAPTER 2

ABRAHAM— HOSPITALITY

I will bless you . . . and all peoples on earth will be blessed through you.

GEN. 12:2–3

The old man sat at the entrance of his tent, the sun nearing its crest, as the day grew hotter. He had watched a hundred years tick by, yet these small hours were pregnant with potential. Abraham had a promise—a God-promise: "I will bless [your wife Sarah] and will surely give you a son by her" (Gen. 17:16). But God left after making that seemingly impossible promise, and so Abraham sat at the entrance of his tent like all old men do, thinking of days gone by and hoping that enough time lay before him to see his dreams realized.

Then he saw them; three men stood near enough to his tent for him to discern they were God's messengers, yet far enough away that he desired to draw nearer to them. Standing, then running, the aged sage greeted the messengers, bowing low before them and saying, "If I have found favor in your eyes, my lord, do not pass your servant by. Let a little water be brought, and then you may all wash your feet and rest under this tree. Let me get you something to eat, so you can be refreshed and then go on your way" (Gen. 18:3–5). The men obliged.

Abraham raced into his tent, exclaiming to Sarah, "Quick . . . get three *seahs* of the finest flour and knead it and bake some bread" (Gen. 18:6). Then running to his herd, Abraham selected the most prized calf for preparation and, when it was ready, he set it before his visitors along with milk and curds, waiting on them as they reclined under a tree and enjoyed the meal. One of the guests vocalized what Abraham hoped to hear. "I will surely return to you about this time next year, and Sarah your wife will have a son" (v. 10).

Notice how the writer narrated the scene: he *ran* to meet the visitors; he *hastened* into the tent and called Sarah to act *quickly*; he *ran* to the herd; he *stood* near them as they sat, all toward one goal—he *waited* on the visitors.

Hospitality encapsulates Abraham's essence in a word, revealing one aspect of what it means to be made in God's image. He is a picture of fierce and over-the-top hospitality. The old man races to and fro, perhaps moving at speeds he had not reached since his youth. He understands hospitality, and he hopes for God's promises. And because he does, God's promise is confirmed and enacted through a total stranger.[4]

Basic Belief: Money Should Be Used to Make Others Feel Special and Valued

Abraham types use money and other resources—however much or little—as opportunities to show God's loving-kindness to others. They view their personal resources, which are tangible expressions of their money, as means to bless others because that is part of why they, like Abraham, exist. "All nations on earth will be blessed through him" (Gen. 18:18). They realize the blessings they've personally received afford an opportunity to prepare a table full of choice food for a stranger or friend, sheltering them from life's pressures at the hearth of their hospitality—and doing this brings them fulfillment.

Abraham types, who are very others-centered with their approach to money, don't use their resources for the purpose of drawing attention to themselves, but to point to the goodness of God while at the same time encouraging the hearts of the ones receiving. Serving others with resources is not an act of drudgery for this type.

Essentially, Abraham types reveal the hospitality of God, the One who desires to care for and comfort his children with special kindness. Abraham types go out of their way and over the top to make certain those in their sphere of influence feel valued, accepted, and empowered, and they use the full force of their resources to send this message.

When I think of Abraham types, my friends Naomi and Rich come to mind. Many years ago, my wife, Elizabeth, and I were in student ministry. One night we scheduled a boys' athletic event at the church and a girls' sleepover at our home. My event with the boys ended late in the evening, and since my home was flooded to the rafters with estrogen, Elizabeth and I agreed I should spend the night elsewhere.

I remembered a couple in our church who were nearing retirement and had invited my wife and me over for dinner on a couple of occasions. We were never able to join them, but I thought this would be a good chance to take them up on their offer to come to their home. It would also keep me from having to sleep in my front yard to avoid being home while girls giggled into all hours of the night, watched *The Princess Bride*, and painted one another's toenails—a fate worse than death, in my mind.

I called Naomi and Rich.

"Naomi! Hello, this is Pastor Tommy from church. You may have seen in the bulletin on Sunday that we're having simultaneous events for the youth tonight—the girls with Elizabeth and the boys with me. Well, the girls are coming over to our place tonight, and I was wondering—"

I didn't get to finish my sales pitch. Naomi knew where I was going and spared me the embarrassment of having to admit I had planned poorly and wanted to crash on their couch.

"Sure, dear. What time will you be arriving?"

"Sometime around 9:30 p.m."

"That's just perfect. Rich and I will be in bed by then, but you just come on over. I'll leave the light on for you and a key under the mat."

I pulled into their driveway around ten o'clock. All youth group events run late, every time. Their front yard was lit like the White House. I parked my car on the paved runway in their front yard and walked to the front door as small motion-detecting lights popped on one by one with what seemed like every step. I saw a piece of paper on a table beside the front door. Unfolding it, I admired the stationery, the crispness of the fold, and the weight of the paper. It stated, "Your room is ready for you. When you enter, take the hall to the left, then turn right. Your room is straight ahead."

I stole down the hallway and recognized my room. A small lamp splashed a graceful, golden hue upon the walls. Resting my backpack on the floor, I noticed a bottle of water sitting inside an ice bucket filled to the brim with fresh ice, and a cup that sat beside the ice bucket. Another note, this time inside an envelope, presented itself beside the water. "Your restroom is down the hall on the right. Breakfast will be ready at 8:00 a.m. Feel free to join us whenever you desire."

In the restroom a hand towel rested beside a small scented candle that flickered and was reflected in the mirror. Never before had a restroom appeared beautiful to me. Everything was just right.

When morning followed a deep, restful sleep, I joined Naomi and Rich in their breakfast nook. They were sitting at the table, sharing cups of coffee, with scribbled notes on small pieces of paper before them, all surrounding their Bible.

Rich smiled and offered me some breakfast—orange juice or milk, whole wheat bread or a bagel, eggs scrambled or over easy, oatmeal or grits, bacon or ham? I sat down with Naomi while Rich prepared my short order.

Then a small but energetic voice burst into the room, cracking the serenity. "Grandma! Grandpa!" the boy cried. His mother followed behind him.

"This is our grandson," said Naomi, "and this is our daughter. They stayed with us last night as well."

I wondered how many others had lodged at their home last night. As I gathered my belongings to walk to my car and leave, they invited me back—anytime. I assured them I would return.

Core Characteristics of Abraham Types

EXCEED EXPECTATIONS

Abraham promised his mysterious guests a *little* water and a *morsel* of bread; he delivered a full-course meal from the choicest of his stock—the best he had to give. Similarly, Abraham types go above and beyond what is promised or even expected to ensure that others have not only what they need, but also what they desire. Abraham types underpromise and overdeliver because they see money as a great resource to make an everyday moment, or a person, feel special.

When it comes to money, their first concern is not how far they can stretch a dollar, but rather how they can create pleasurable experiences for others, experiences that surprise and delight. For example, when invited to gatherings, instead of bringing a four-dollar vegetable tray, if they can afford it, Abraham types will likely show up with a rack of ribs and a couple of sides. Abraham types rarely consider what they can do to simply check the box, to meet expectations. Instead they thoughtfully contemplate the perfect gift, meal, or other contribution that will let the recipient know this moment was not merely thrown together, but was tailor-made especially for them. Because of this core characteristic, Abraham types will commonly spend a larger-than-usual portion of their incomes on meals, gifts, or other means of showing exceptional hospitality.

PUT OTHERS FIRST

Abraham types are others-focused, even to the point of putting their own desires last. We see an example of this in Genesis 13:8–9. Because their livestock had become too great for both of them to settle in the same area, Abraham gave Lot first option of all the land that lay before them; Abraham took what Lot didn't want.

When it comes to money, Abraham types will expend immense energy to make certain others get what they want, often at their own expense, and occasionally to their own self-neglect. You may not hear them say it, but they are often thinking, "I feel guilty when I get what I want and spend money on myself." They'll spend on others, but when it comes to personal expenditures for their own pleasure, generally those take a backseat to everything else.

Meredith and Ashley, sisters who are now raising families of their own, sat in our home one evening as we studied the seven money types. Meredith strongly resonated with the Abraham type, and she expressed how she often puts other people's desires ahead of her own. She shared a typical shopping scenario.

"Let's say I'm walking the aisles of a store and I see a purse I really like. My first thought is not that I should get it for myself; my first thought is that I should get it for my sister, Ashley." Ashley smiled as we all laughed, but this inclination for an Abraham type is very real—they're often so focused on other people's desires and happiness that their own enjoyment is suppressed.

Abraham types can learn to take advantage of their giving nature while not being taken advantage of. Showing hospitality to others through the way they use money is refreshing for this type, but also presents the risk of wearing them out, or opening their lives to those who would drain them of resources or energy. This others-focused orientation is wonderful and scripturally affirmed. However, if taken to the extreme, forgoing one's own well-being for the benefit of another can have harmful effects, leading to burnout, exhaustion, and despair. While they draw much energy and joy from serving and hosting others, the flow of hospitality coming from their lives will eventually drain them if they don't take time to replenish.

BELIEVE GIVING IS A GIFT

Ask those who walk the way of Abraham and they will tell you it truly is more blessed to give than receive. By giving to another person or organization, something awakens in an Abraham type's inner life that doesn't through any other daily activity. Because they are often unable to fully explain what is transpiring, you might hear Abraham types say something like, "I get more out of giving than anyone who receives from me gets."

Could Abraham have foreseen how important welcoming the three strangers would be to his life's unfolding story? As we discovered, the strangers Abraham welcomed were actually God's gift of grace to Abraham. In this way Abraham, the host, became the hosted—when Abraham offered a meal to the strangers, they delivered God's promise of a son to him.

Abraham types approach money with a boomerang mentality. They believe they can always release the resources in their hands because more is coming their way. This type tends not to stress about money as much as some other types; they believe God will provide for them in the same way they provide for others; they live in an economic cycle of trust, and so they lead very open-handed, generous lives.

Use Resources to Serve in Often Unnoticed Ways

Over the course of my work in pastoral ministry, I often overlooked one of the most wonderful gifts to our faith community—Abraham types. They're not likely to jump up and down and clamor for attention or present themselves in pushy ways. They're not usually high-maintenance individuals. They're often behind the scenes, waiting to be asked to help with something that truly makes a difference in another person's day.

My mother, Alisha, is a great example of this characteristic. Having attended church as a young girl, but only sporadically since then, she started coming to church to hear me preach to teenage students. Eventually she wanted to help.

I inquired, "What do you want to do?"

She responded, "Whatever you need."

Well, I knew my mother couldn't carry a tune in a bucket, her tech skills stopped with checking email, and she was too nice to provide crowd control. Basically, I didn't have a role for her. Then she had an idea.

"You know those generic birthday cards you send out to students in their birthday month? Why don't you let me take that over? Get me a list of the birthdays and I'll buy the cards—just help me pick something out students will like."

Every week my mother scoured the student ministry's list of several hundred teens and made sure each received a birthday card in the mail. Their names were handwritten on the card, along with an encouraging thought based on our knowledge of the students. She personalized a mechanized process that students likely saw right through. My mother is a classic Abraham type, always ready to go above and beyond to make others feel welcomed and special.

Abraham types will use their money, much like my mother did, to make certain others feel special and have what they need. I know one Abraham type who coordinates the nursery program at his church. Rather than asking the church to pay for wet wipes and crackers for the little ones, he spends his personal allowance to provide the resources, so as not to financially burden the church. To Abraham types, these sorts of expenditures are no big deal, even if the cost is significant in their own budgets. It's unlikely they will tell anyone they are making these purchases; people will just assume that, week after week, these supplies magically appear. Because they prefer to use resources to serve others in a way that doesn't draw attention to themselves, Abraham types are just fine with people making these types of assumptions.

Enjoy Using Food to Show Kindness

We've witnessed how Abraham provided food for his guests, and how that led to his guests blessing him in return. It's common that Abraham types use their resources to demonstrate hospitality to others with meals.

I once had the privilege of witnessing a subtle, seemingly insignificant act of generosity from an Abraham type come full circle, which revealed God's hospitality to someone in a significant way. Reed loves to cook; he comes to life in the kitchen. Some people paint, others make music. Reed creates food that makes your mouth water. Many nights, by the time his family leaves the table, most everything he prepared has disappeared into the bottoms of their bellies.

But one night Reed had plenty of leftover spaghetti. The thought occurred to him, "I should take this food up to the church; someone may need it." So, having never done this before, he packaged the spaghetti into a container and delivered it to the church office. He didn't think another thing about what he'd done. He picked up the container the next week and went about his life.

Seven years later we hosted both Reed and a young woman in our home. As we dialogued over coffee, the young woman became somewhat choked up, saying, "I've never told you this before, Reed, but do you remember when you delivered spaghetti to the church a long time ago? I found out it was you from the receptionist." After racking his brain for a moment, Reed vaguely recalled the scenario. The woman continued, "You had no way of knowing this, but at that time I was barely paying my bills, and I didn't have any money left over for food that particular week. I was crying out to the Lord in prayer to help me get food, and I didn't want to tell anyone I was struggling.

"That same day the receptionist sent an email to a group of

people with whom I was volunteering at the church, telling us there was spaghetti in the break room. Nobody else stopped by to get any, so at the day's end, I took it home with me. I ate that spaghetti all week. It was just enough to get me through until payday."

Every eye in the room welled up with tears. The young woman thanked Reed, ending with a powerful statement: "You delivered the spaghetti, but for me, it was straight from God." Reed was merely doing what he loved, sharing the resources God gave him, hoping they would brighten someone's day. However, what he may not have realized at the time is that God often moves about, unnoticed, through hospitable acts. God's love is realized when Abraham types, like Reed, use their resources to show kindness to others. Abraham types may never understand the impact their acts of hospitality make, but for those recipients with eyes to see and ears to hear, God's presence is often felt because of what they do.

Shadow Side: Self-Sufficiency

Every type has a shadow side, but remember, every shadow requires the presence of some light—even the shadow side has some goodness with it. The shadow side of the Abraham type is self-sufficiency, the belief that help is not needed from others, an attitude of *I'm fine; don't worry about me.* Those who are most inclined to bless others may have a hard time receiving blessings, and may develop a mindset of superiority—always the helper, never the helped.

If this shadow side is not addressed, it will morph an Abraham type's hospitality—an others-centered approach to making people feel special by using resources—into a self-serving attempt to assuage an internal longing to feel needed, to become powerful, and even to feel superior to others.

DIFFICULTY RECEIVING GENEROSITY FROM OTHERS

We see aspects of this shadow side in operation in Abraham's life in Genesis 14:13–24, when his nephew Lot was kidnapped. Abraham learned this news when a person who had escaped the hostility fled and informed him. Then Abraham summoned his men and counted them; 318 assembled and received their orders. They attacked at nightfall and reclaimed the stolen possessions and their kin.

King Bera of Sodom met Abraham in the Valley of the King. Melchizedek, king and priest of Salem, brought out bread and wine, blessing Abraham, and Abraham gave him a tenth of everything he retrieved from the battle. Hearing the blessing, seeing the exchange, King Bera told Abraham, "Give me the people and keep the goods for yourself" (v. 21). Abraham refused, saying, "I will accept nothing belonging to you, not even a thread or the strap of a sandal, so that you will never be able to say, 'I made Abram rich'" (v. 23). Perhaps Abraham didn't want to get mixed up with the likes of the king of Sodom. However, a close study of Abraham's life reveals a refusal to receive resources occurred more than once in his life (see also Genesis 23 when Abraham refused free land upon which to bury his wife).

Have you known people who were always doing good for others, but when you noticed a need in their lives, your help was refused? One Abraham type expressed that she was uncomfortable at her own baby shower when others gave her gifts because she felt indebted or beholden to them, as though now they held some power over her and she was obligated to get them a gift in return— for no specific occasion, but merely to settle the score. This woman, however, has no problem going to any baby shower or other special occasion and lavishing gifts on another.

Sometimes an Abraham type will wrestle with being on the receiving end of generosity. It can even make some feel weak, not in control, and deficient. If they're really honest, some Abraham types who wrestle with their shadow sides will tell you they like being the one always providing for others because it makes them feel needed. This form of self-sufficiency can be rooted in deep-seated insecurity, which is essentially a thinly veiled form of pride.

SLIPPING INTO A MINDSET OF SUPERIORITY

Another aspect of an Abraham type's shadow side is a belief that the person receiving acts of hospitality or benevolence is somehow inferior to the person providing it. In other words, it's easy to think, "I'm helping you, therefore I'm better." True hospitality with resources is not about *helping* someone; rather, it's about *honoring* someone. When Abraham received his special guests, he respected them with his words (*calling them my lords*), with his posture (*bowing down before them*), and with his resources (*providing the very best*). Realizing he was ultimately a person passing through life, dependent upon God's hospitality and provision, Abraham served his guests. It's a good thing he did. As can be seen as the story unfolds, Abraham's guests carried with them a special message and the power to bless the man who hosted them. Granted, not every exchange with a guest is as dramatic as this one, yet every guest does bear divine significance because each person bears the image of God, is inherently equal, and has the right to be treated with dignity and respect, regardless of gender, ethnicity, or socioeconomic status.

Growing in Financial Well-Being

Embrace Your Desire to Show Hospitality

Culture may lead you to believe you're not good with money unless you make it all about you. Perhaps you've even thought you're bad with money because you spend a lot of it on other people, rather than building your own empire. Take confidence in knowing that your sense of financial fulfillment will not come as it does for other people—you find meaning with money by using it hospitably to pour love onto others. Embrace this aspect of your personal makeup as God's design in your life.

Living as an Abraham type isn't easy. You're often focused on what other people want and need, and there's never a shortage of people who need something from you. You may occasionally think you exist entirely for other people, and if you allow yourself to wear that mantle, that may become true. But this need not be the case. Embrace your others-centered approach to money from the perspective that God has designed you to be a vessel through which divine love is expressed with how you use money, not as someone who is somehow inferior to others and must spend money to make others happy. You matter because God has uniquely designed you, and God designed you specifically to reveal his image.

Check Your Motives

Before spending money on others, check your motives. Are you making this purchase because you want to express your love and care for another person, or do you somehow feel obliged, as though you owe it to them? Always give and spend from a place of confidence and never in hopes that your gift or other acts of generosity will somehow elicit a response. You'll only set yourself up for disappointment. Remember, people may come to expect your hospitality; they may become accustomed to living in the glow of your gifts. Then their lack of showing appreciation can become your question of self-worth. If you find yourself giving to make others happy or to gain their approval, shelve your hospitality and return to a place of inner confidence. Return to the hospitality of God's love toward you. Then you'll overflow with generosity, needing nothing in return, for you have been filled by God's love.

Ask Others What They Want

You're generally in tune with what other people want and need, but you need to remain cognizant that acts of hospitality are received differently by others. Consider asking your intended recipients what they want or need, rather than assuming you know best. If they refuse your hospitality, this is not a reflection on you or your ability to discern what they desire. People reject God's good gifts in their lives all the time; you're in good company. You'll honor your recipients by seeking to understand what they desire, rather than assuming you always know best.

Tell Others What You Want

You spend your life using money to make others feel special, and you need to help the rest of us know how we can use our money to make you feel special. When we ask you where you want to go for dinner, on vacation, for the weekend, or out on a date, we need you to tell us what you want—not what you think we want you to want. This sounds simple for most types, but for Abraham types, it may be difficult because they're most concerned that everyone else gets what they want. You'll do the rest of us a great service by telling us what you want. If it helps you feel any better, consider this one more way you serve us! You'll save the rest of us the agony of trying to read your mind.

ESTABLISH A BUDGET FOR HOSPITALITY EXPENDITURES

Hospitality without a budget is like a river without banks—too many resources flowing without boundaries can actually do more harm than good. The world's needs always overwhelm your capacity to give. On occasion Abraham types may completely blow the budget (if they have one) that was allocated toward giving gifts, throwing parties, entertaining others, supporting charities, and other hospitable endeavors. Abraham types might consider setting a strict budget for these types of expenditures, perhaps even withdrawing the budgeted amount in cash each month and only spending that set amount.

If Abraham types cannot properly manage finances because they regularly overspend on hospitable acts, this constrains the opportunities for God to partner with them to demonstrate loving-kindness via finances. This will cause Abrahamic souls no small amount of pain as they pass up opportunities to show hospitality. In these cases, consider two things. First, there may be ways to accomplish the same purpose without much, or any, money. Second, remember that you are not the world's only host. Can others in your life partner with you to accomplish some desired purpose?

REMEMBER TO SPEND ON YOURSELF

Your shadow side and others-centered orientation leads you to neglect proper self-care. You can guard against this shadow side by remembering to be good to yourself with your finances. I learned this lesson from a prominent Abraham type.

I once mailed a tattered copy of a book to its author in hopes he would inscribe it with a personal note for my son and then return it. I included a self-addressed, stamped envelope. Two weeks later, I received two copies of the book in return, both autographed—my tattered copy and a fresh, mint copy. I opened the cover of the new book and found the following inscription to my son: "Seth, be good to yourself." This is wonderful advice for an Abraham type.

Because you often care for the needs of everyone around you, you may pay little attention to your own desires. You need to responsibly plan to occasionally splurge on yourself. Set aside some expendable money each month just for the purpose of indulging in some experience you enjoy. Create a line item in your budget called "Me," no matter how small it is, and spend the money on yourself. If it helps, imaginatively step outside yourself and view yourself as the other person to whom you so often show kindness and love. Creatively plan and budget for a day trip or afternoon just to be good to yourself. Put as much thought into it as you would if you were planning the trip for a dear friend. If you need to, enlist a friend to plan the outing with you. Then, do it!

While it may seem extravagant to spend so much energy on yourself, this is part of remaining healthy as an Abraham type. Then, if you're out shopping and see an item you like, rather than thinking about someone else you can buy it for, buy it for yourself!

You may have heard the Scripture "Love your neighbor as yourself," which appears in several places in the Bible. Part of loving your neighbor well is learning to demonstrate love to yourself, and part of loving yourself is being good to yourself. Do this with joy and without guilt. Abraham types, you make us feel valuable; please be certain to notice how valuable you are as well.

From Guilt to Joy: An Abraham Type Embraces Her Design

When Francesca awakened to the reality that God designed her to use money to make others feel special, that she was an Abraham type, she recovered the sense of joy and purpose she felt early in life—a joy she had lost for a season of time. Her whole life Francesca loved using her money to make others feel important and noticed. Birthday money went to buying her mother earrings; allowance was regularly spent on items for siblings and friends at school. As an adult, however, she was taught that she needed to be tighter with her money, putting it to better use, especially by saving and investing for her future.

It's not that Francesca was frivolous with her finances. She had enough in savings to cover emergency expenses and was funding her retirement account on a monthly basis, but she was told she could be doing even more. She felt guilty because she thought she wasn't properly using her money if she spent it on others. More than that, she felt unfulfilled financially.

For years she wrestled with financial angst, the tension created when your soul longs for one thing, but culture—or those around you—affirms another. When Francesca discovered her money type, it was like years of guilt peeled away. Through tears she expressed that she always loved using her money to show hospitality. Now she continues to fund her retirement, but she also funds the local food bank each month with much-needed supplies and money to do their good work in the community—and she does it with joy.

🌿 A BLESSING FOR ABRAHAM TYPES 🌿

*We see God in you because of the ways you make us feel special
and deeply loved; our hearts are warmed in the glow of your
hospitality. You demonstrate to us that we matter to God,
reminding us that his eye is upon us, just as it is upon a spar-
row, which is fed at the table of God's generous hospitality,
day by day. We're accepted just as we are when we're in your
presence. When we look at you, we catch a glimpse of the
image of God, who loves beyond what is expected or deserved
and serves us in ways that surprise us each day. You, by the
ways you use money hospitably, help us see God a little clearer.
You help us feel his love. Your acts of generosity remind us of
God's hospitality, pointing us to the One who prepares a table
for us and leads us by still waters.*

🌿 SCRIPTURES FOR THE HOSPITABLE SOUL 🌿

Read the following Scriptures, each accompanied by words to personalize this exercise. Notice the Scripture you resonate with the
most. Then softly read it aloud several times, write it out, and ponder it until you can almost recall it from memory. Over the coming
days, find affirmation in knowing that you bring God's love into
the world in meaningful ways, and that the Scriptures affirm your
way of being in the world related to resources.

- I am on this earth to "share with the Lord's people who are
  in need" and to "practice hospitality" (Rom. 12:13).
- I have been given the privilege to "offer hospitality." As
  I have received this gift, I will use it to "serve others," as
  a faithful steward of "God's grace in its various forms"
  (1 Peter 4:9–10).

✍ My love toward others reminds them of God's loving-
kindness as he "graciously gives us all things" (Rom. 8:32).

✌ REFLECTION QUESTIONS FOR ABRAHAM TYPES ✌

✍ How do you use money hospitably? How does this make
you feel?

✍ Who else in your life is an Abraham type?

✍ Which of the core characteristics or stories about Abraham
or Abraham types did you most resonate with and why?
How do you see yourself in light of this characteristic or
story?

✍ Do you experience financial tension with certain people?
If so, in what way might your Abraham money type
contribute to this tension?

✍ What is one thing you plan to do differently with money
now that you understand your Abraham money type?

✍ What is the greatest truth you've learned about the
Abraham money type?

CHAPTER 3

ISAAC—DISCIPLINE

[Isaac] moved on from there and dug another well.
GEN. 26:22

Conditions in the land grew bleak. Farmers and herdsmen had a word for when times got this bad, a word they hated to use but knew was reality—*famine*. Everything in their world depended on the land, and as went the land, so went the prosperity of the people.

This was no time for travel, but famine afforded no options. Isaac had to find a place to settle and survive, and so he traced his late father's footsteps into Gerar, Philistine territory. Like Abraham did during famine, Isaac considered heading for Egypt. God had blessed Abraham in times like these, and so Isaac mirrored his father's actions, hoping God's promise to Abraham of becoming a great people in a well-nourished land would carry into his own life. Then God directed Isaac, saying, "Do not go down to Egypt; live in the land where I tell you to live. Stay in this land for a while, and I will be with you and will bless you" (Gen. 26:2–3).

"This land" was not exactly an optimal place to stay. The fertile Egyptian crescent with its Nile floodplains and rich soil provided better conditions for planting. Further, Philistine neighbors offered no assurance of support for Isaac's sojourning kinsmen; settling here was neither optimal nor logical, and posed no small amount of danger to his family. While Abraham's trek into Egypt was no sure path to survival, it appeared a sight better than weathering the lack of rainfall and water sources in Gerar. At least in Egypt there was water. Instead of leading Isaac down the most logical path, God directed him to where only God could provide, where amid famine and opposition God's provision would be magnified.

The stakes were intimidating; odds stacked high against Isaac. It's tough to summon the courage and discipline necessary to sow seed in a famine. If you plant, you risk losing whatever seed you have. If you don't plant, you're certain to reap nothing. Everything was on the line, and Isaac needed the most optimal conditions for sustaining livelihood. However, against reason, clinging only to God's promise, Isaac remained and planted. The results were staggering.

> Isaac planted crops in that land and the same year reaped a hundredfold, because the Lord blessed him. The man became rich, and his wealth continued to grow until he became very wealthy. He had so many flocks and herds and servants that the Philistines envied him. (Gen. 26:12–14)

Directed by promise, guided by a sense of destiny, and yet wrestling with conditions that forecasted certain demise, Isaac took what he had, entrusted it to God, and with God's help made the most of limited resources and opportunities.

It's important to point out that God's promises and provision in Isaac's life, amid his planting and reaping a hundredfold in a famine, did not remove resistance. If the road toward worthwhile goals was easy, one would not need discipline. Therefore, Isaac's story would hold no lesson for us in this regard. This fact, however, is clear in the passage above: when the Philistines saw his success, they envied and resisted him. God's blessings attracted conflict (see Gen. 26:14 and the following verses). These tensions of comingled blessings and resistances, opportunities and setbacks, are the places where discipline emerges as a guiding force that compels a person toward opportunity.

As we'll see, discipline marked Isaac's life, demonstrating a quality of divine image. Isaac embodies a determination to make the most of whatever is at his disposal, reminding us that God takes all things, however bleak the situation, and works them together for the good. Nothing is wasted.

Basic Belief: Money Should Be Maximized

Isaac types are focused and determined with their finances, seeking to make the most of their resources. The God who redeems even the direst situations, who makes the most of resources countless times in the Scriptures when his people experience lack, is revealed through the disciplined mindsets and actions of Isaac types. Isaac types see potential in all things because with God anything is possible. Therefore, nothing is wasted—everything is maximized.

If you give Isaac types a dollar, they will do their best to turn it into ten, not because they like making money, but because of an inner determination to maximize potential. It is crucially important to delineate between self-centered multiplication and maximization, and it all comes down to motivation. Isaac types are not motivated by a sense of *more is better* in and of itself, but by a sense of *most*—that is, maximizing resources so the most possible good and potential use of the resources results.

Isaac types likely have a strong desire to know where their money is going. Their budgets are generally organized, and they have a plan that takes into account their future financial needs. They'll analyze their budgets to make certain they are maximizing their resources, often inflicting tight, self-imposed financial restrictions on themselves, limiting the amount of money they (or others sharing their budgets) will spend on personal enjoyment or seemingly frivolous endeavors.

At their best, Isaac types' discipline is based in a mindset that longs to bring honor to the Lord because they take so seriously the resources he has entrusted to their care. They think, "I must make the most of this because God has placed this money within my sphere of influence." They view themselves as God's partners in bringing about good in the world by how they use money, so not one dime is wasted. They even find ways to monetize the most normal, everyday experiences and objects in life, seeing potential to maximize resources in ways others overlook.

Joseph Bullin is a clear example of an Isaac type. For as long as I've known him, he's started celebrating Christmas in July. It's strange to some, but sort of funny to see no less than half a dozen Christmas trees lit in his home during the summer months and all through fall. Who else does this? He loves Christmas, and he also loves Christmas ornaments. He's learned when local stores receive, and also discount, their Christmas ornaments. He's tapped into, of all things, a Christmas ornament market and buys rare and under-valued ornaments and sells them online for a remarkable profit. With that money he's able to travel the country and enjoy the open road. While not dipping into his regular income from his day job, he maximizes his *extra* money.

You'll find this trait in many Isaac types: they see potential to make a profit where others see "a mere ornament." And, they'll view this money as extra money, avoiding, as much as possible, touching their regular incomes. They'll rely on this supplemental income for trips, desired purchases, and nonessentials.

Core Characteristics of Isaac Types

DISCIPLINED TOWARD DESTINY

Like his father, Abraham, Isaac lived with a profound sense of destiny, that something more awaited him. God told Isaac, "Through your offspring all nations on earth will be blessed" (Gen. 26:4). This sense of promise and opportunity enables Isaac types to stand firm in the face of opposition and remain disciplined toward a preferred financial future. Even in the face of great adversity, they persist toward their *why*, like the promise the Lord made to Isaac. It guides them, and nothing stands in their way en route to achieving their goals. They'll take whatever is thrown at them, figure out what to do with it, and deploy their resources toward their desired ends.

When Elizabeth and I were newly married, we learned the power of being financially disciplined, and it changed our financial future. More than that, though I didn't have language for it at the time, I realized my strongest inclinations were that of an Isaac type.

We dreamed of a day when Elizabeth would be able to stay at home and focus on raising our children. Our finances seemed to conspire against us to keep that from happening. With college loans, medical bills, and car payments, we were approximately thirty thousand dollars in debt and reality hit us—we did not have enough money for Elizabeth to quit her job. She being a teacher and I being a youth minister, we were not living high on the hog. We saw no clear way to change our financial situation. The way we saw it, we had two options: keep doing the same things and hope for a different result (which is often cited as one way to define insanity) or ask for help and try something new.

Swallowing our pride, we asked a minister at our church to help us figure out what we should do. Scheduling that appointment was one of the most humbling and embarrassing experiences of my life. Money was something we did not talk about, especially when we realized we were not making enough of it to do what we wanted to do, or so we thought.

We walked into Ed's office nervous and ashamed. It felt like we were about to get a physical at the hands of one of my coworkers. In some sense, that's what it was—a financial physical. Ed poked and prodded every crack and crevice of our financial situation. Then he looked up from the documents and asked a question that altered our outlook. "So why do you want to change your financial situation?"

I answered, "We want Elizabeth to be able to stay home and raise our children."

"If your *why* is strong enough, you'll endure *whatever* you need to, to reach your goal," he said. Then he instructed us to keep our receipts for thirty days and check back with him.

We had our first assignment. We kept every receipt for the next month, and when our check-up date arrived, we emptied a paper bag full of little white strips of paper onto his desk. We separated them into categories: groceries, transportation, utilities, entertainment, and so on. Ed opened a spreadsheet that looked like something NASA would have created and typed in a few numbers pertaining to our loan payments, interest rates, and receipt amounts. He delivered the diagnosis: "You can be debt free in one year."

I smiled and looked at Elizabeth and said, "Did you hear that? I'm getting a raise!" Ed laughed and explained that although I was not getting a raise, if we would become intentional about how we spent our money, we could pay off all our debt in about thirteen months.

Ed gave us clear, practical, and actionable steps to reach our goal. The rest was up to us. Was our *why* strong enough? For the next year we disciplined ourselves, lived on a tight budget, attacked debt with every extra penny we found or earned, and in just a little over eleven months we retired all the debt—one month ahead of schedule. Our *why* was indeed strong enough, and we disciplined ourselves to persist through *whatever* came our way. It wasn't easy, but it was worth it.

The most important word we learned that year was *no*. We said things like, "No, we're sorry, we can't go out to dinner and a movie with you, but do you want to come over and watch a movie in our home?" Now, we didn't say no to everything, but we did say no to whatever would stop us from saying yes to Elizabeth being able to stay home when we started a family. We learned what it meant to be financially disciplined toward a goal, realizing that a good plan, a clear goal, and discipline can carry willing people toward incredible results.

Greg McKeown articulates the struggle clearly when he writes, "To eliminate nonessentials means saying *no* to someone. Often. It means pushing against social expectations. To do it well takes courage *and* compassion. So eliminating the nonessentials isn't just about mental discipline. It's about the *emotional discipline* necessary to say no to social pressure."[5] Finding your why, eliminating nonessentials, and keeping your eye on your desired goal gives you the fortitude to remain financially disciplined toward your dream.

SEE POTENTIAL FOR RECOVERY AND RESTORATION

Good enough is simply not good enough for Isaac types. This is not because Isaac types demand perfection, but because they see potential. We clearly see the image of God breaking through an Isaac type's life in this aspect. God takes what is in disrepair, bringing beauty from ashes, and works with us to restore the brokenness around us.

When Isaac types see potential, they analyze resources and align them toward maximum impact. In Genesis 26:18 we read, "Isaac reopened the wells that had been dug in the time of his father Abraham, which the Philistines had stopped up after Abraham died, and he gave them the same names his father had given them." It's interesting that Isaac renamed the wells his father Abraham dug long ago with the original names his father gave them. These were more than wells; they were markers of God's provision to a previous generation, and Isaac restored what was lost. Isaac reclaimed the dignity of the wells the Philistines damaged.

Isaac types see potential, whether in a program, an object, or a person, and they're inclined to take whatever is before them and develop it. To that end, Isaac types recover what is in disrepair; they restore damaged assets. Isaac types ask, "What is the potential here?" of things others undervalue. They refuse to allow opportunity to remain untapped. Isaac types have a thorough understanding of reality as it is, and yet refuse to abandon reality as it can become. They keep the future in mind and pour all their energies into making sure they maximize everything within their control.

Tom Cousins's work in the East Lake community is a case in point. The East Lake community once skirted Atlanta like a summer dress on a bright-eyed little girl, but by 1960 the resort community had devolved into a crime-ridden ghetto. In his book *Toxic Charity*, Robert Lupton recounts the situation: Property values had plummeted, businesses had left, drugs and prostitution flourished. As Lupton records, Tom Cousins, a successful real estate developer, saw the potential upside of the community amid all its ruin. Partnering with like-minded agencies and business associates, he identified the three most crime-ridden spots in the community—"two streets where criminal activity was nearly unchecked and, right in the middle of the neighborhood, a 650-unit public-housing project."

Soon the one-time hot spot of criminal activity, the dilapidated apartment complex, was demolished and replaced, offering citizens quality and affordable housing under new ownership. Next the group focused their attention on the educational challenges that would have to be met if the tide would turn in that community. After being granted a charter school for East Lake, within two years student performance in the school rose from rock bottom to third among public schools in Atlanta.

The financial engine that fueled the East Lake turnaround was not actually a restored housing community or the incredible revolution in education, but the newly renovated East Lake Golf Course, which welcomed dozens of the nation's most elite business people to join the club. As of this writing, you can flip on the television every September and see East Lake Golf Course hosting the PGA

Tour's final golf tournament of the year. As a champion emerges on the last hole of the Tour Championship each year, those who know East Lake's story and the PGA Tour's charitable spirit realize the real emerging winner is the East Lake community, which receives over one million dollars a year in support for hosting the event. Now East Lake is one of the most desirable communities in the area.[6]

The project's leader, Tom Cousins, walked the way of Isaac as he envisioned a new future for the East Lake community. He could not have generated the level of support from local authorities and the PGA Tour had the project simply been another real estate development deal. Vision drove the project—vision that restored streets with proper dwellings and an education system to support the economic and community growth. Isaac types see the potential to recover and restore what has been lost or needs repair, not only for themselves, but for their communities.

PERSISTENT IN THE FACE OF RESISTANCE

In Genesis 26:19–22 we read:

> Isaac's servants dug in the valley and discovered a well of fresh water there. But the herders of Gerar quarreled with those of Isaac and said, "The water is ours!" So he named the well Esek, because they disputed with him. Then they dug another well, but they quarreled over that one also; so he named it Sitnah. He moved on from there and dug another well, and no one quarreled over it. He named it Rehoboth, saying, "Now the LORD has given us room and we will flourish in the land."

After re-digging his father's wells, Isaac dug new wells. Seeking to deter him, neighboring people began claiming water rights.

Isaac named two of his new wells, over which these people argued with him, Esek (meaning "dispute") and Sitnah (meaning "opposition"), labeling them based on the difficult experiences of digging them. While continually facing resistance, Isaac moved on and kept digging, looking for an undisputed place to increase in the land, which would allow his family room to flourish. Even though Isaac was mightier than his foes (Gen. 26:16), he demonstrated restraint and kept looking for God's provision, until he eventually dug a new well and named it Rehoboth, meaning "broad places." The tight confines of famine gave way to the broad places of blessing as Isaac persisted toward his promise.

Troublesome conditions are no match for an Isaac type's God-inspired persistence. From the single mom who manages a lean budget as she works two jobs to put food on the table to the millionaire who sees the value in community development even above portfolio development, Isaac types come in all financial shapes and sizes. The thread that binds Isaac types together is not a certain kind of project, personality, sector of operation, or net worth. The thread is discipline that won't quit, a persistence compelling them to *re-dig wells* because they are looking for a broad and sustainable space to allow their families room to flourish. They will not relent until they get what they believe is God's very best for them.

Max is an Isaac type who embodies persistence in the face of resistance. For years I watched him clean the church's facilities after he finished his other full-time job. Once, as I was leaving for the day, I bumped into him in the hallway as he was coming in to work at the church. Max was especially jovial; his fast-paced tenor voice lifted another key as I inquired as to the reason for the wide-eyed grin on his face.

"It's almost done. The house, it'll be finished this week," he exclaimed. We'd never discussed that he was building a house, so I was intrigued as Max described the home's layout, building materials, floor plan, and vast acreage. When Max finished describing his dream home, he described his dream.

"I've always wanted land, a place where my children and one day their children could roam freely. And my wife and I've always wanted enough space for each child to have his or her own room. Now it's almost finished."

I'd never seen Max in that light before, and I'd never look at him the same way again because of what he said next.

"This is why I work a full-time job and then clean this place on the side. I mean, I love doing what I do here, but my wife and I agreed that for a season, I'd invest a few extra hours a week here so between this job and my other one I would earn enough money to pay for this home—in cash."

Earlier that day I saw a man who cleaned our toilets; a man I always enjoyed and respected. Now I saw a man I couldn't see before, one driven by a dream, encountering financial resistance to that dream, and persisting anyhow. Disciplined persistence, inspired by a dream, helped Max overcome many obstacles and remain focused on his financial goals. At first I couldn't see what motivated him to scrub toilets and mop floors with such enthusiasm and vigor. Now I saw clearly.

SHOW RESTRAINT

As Isaac neared his life's end, he was essentially blind. His wife, Rebekah, knew the time had arrived for Isaac to bless their eldest child, Esau. She concocted a plan whereby her favorite child, their younger son, Jacob, would receive the blessings intended for Esau.

Rebekah instructed Jacob to dress up as his older brother and walk into the room so Isaac, fooled into believing Jacob was Esau, could bless him instead. Her plan succeeded. When Esau arrived and went into the room for Isaac to bless him, the deception was revealed and Isaac was shocked. Nevertheless, he restrained himself from blessing Esau as well, though blessing him was his desire from the start. In that culture the elder son should have received the blessing.

The narrative is tragic, and while there isn't much in this story worth emulating, there is something to be learned from Isaac. The Jewish tradition honors Isaac for showing restraint in this moment, for not going beyond the resources at his disposal, for not blessing Esau after Jacob had already been blessed. Sad as it was, Isaac honored his word to Jacob and showed restraint with Esau. Isaac is praised for this action because he mirrors God's restraint. If God did not show restraint, the world could not contain the deluge of his resources—overpowering love and light. Further, in creating the world and its resources, God demonstrated restraint through the boundaries created, such as in Genesis 1:9, where the waters were gathered together in one place and dry land appeared.

Isaac honored the boundaries he had set; he showed restraint, governing his emotions. Isaac types are not given to emotionalism that leads them to overstep their financial boundaries. I've sat through enough church services and fundraising appeals to understand how communicators draw upon emotions to compel people to give. This is not necessarily deceptive or wrong, because our emotions rightfully play a role in leading our hearts to be generous with our finances. However, an Isaac type is less likely to be persuaded to give because of emotional reasons than some others. Isaacs want to know how the money will be handled and who is in charge of making certain that the resources are properly allocated. And they want to see results. This is crucial to understanding an

Isaac type's motivation toward philanthropic giving: an Isaac type must have a strong sense that the person or entity to which they are giving not only is credible, but will make the most of the donation, just as if the Isaac type were in charge of the money.

While emotion may compel an Isaac type to resonate with a particular goal or giving opportunity, logic will determine if that emotion translates into a gift, or whether restraint will be shown in that situation. This is not the case with all types.

Alan is an Isaac type, while his wife, Cherise, identifies with the Abraham type. One Sunday a missionary visited their church and presented a compelling need for medical units in a third-world country. Cherise was moved to tears, and she and Alan donated several thousand dollars and funded a medical unit, also paying to have it stocked with medicine.

Alan and Cherise heard nothing for months, and after about a year, Alan asked for a report from the missionary on how the clinic was doing. He received some generic information and a poorly shot photo from an American on the ground in that country. Basically, he did not get the sense that his donation had truly made a difference.

Some types give to causes they deem worthy and take no second thought for how the money is actually used. But as an Isaac type, Alan claims before he would consider giving again to this missionary, he would have to see more evidence that his last donation was used for its intended purpose, and that the money was thoroughly maximized. Otherwise, he would show restraint with future donations.

LOVE TO WIN BY GETTING THE BEST DEAL

Once I was invited to play golf with a group of successful businessmen. During a break in the round, one of the men, a wealthy venture capitalist who owned a private jet and three vacation homes, asked the group if we knew how he could upgrade his cellular phone package that was more affordable than the options he'd already found. He was trying to figure out how to save what amounted to a one-time expense of about fifty dollars.

At one point, one of the men asked him, "Are you trying to gas up the plane with that extra fifty dollars you'll save?" The question elicited a roar of laughter, even from the man trying to save the money. This was typical behavior for him, and all his friends knew it and gave him a well-deserved hard time. Whether he was negotiating a cell phone contract or a multi-million-dollar business deal, he treated each transaction like it would break the bank if it went wrong.

This tendency of Isaac types can make them highly successful, and can also cause them to major on minor savings. That one and the same mindset drives them all the time. This mindset stems from the Isaac-type tendency toward maximization, which we see in Isaac's life in the aforementioned examples of re-digging wells. Isaac types love to get the best deal because it feels like winning, and winning lets them know they've made the most of their money. When an Isaac type saves money or gets a deal, they feel like they've won, regardless how insignificant the amount of savings is.

Shadow Side: Fear

Isaac is the first person in the Bible God commands to not be fearful. "I am the God of your father Abraham. Do not be afraid, for I am with you; I will bless you and will increase the number of your descendants for the sake of my servant Abraham" (Gen. 26:24). The Scriptures are good at not wasting words. If God says, "Fear not," it's because fear is present. The heart-level issue that needed to be addressed in Isaac was apparently fear. I'm no psychologist, but if my father had strapped me to a pile of wood and nearly thrust a dagger through my heart, I think I would live with a little trepidation (see Gen. 22:1–24).

Fear morphs disciplined desire to honor God's name by the way we handle finances into miserly management of money, striving, and even greed, for the sake of personal security and self-preservation. There is no way to be at peace with God and money if fear drives the way we relate to finances. Love and fear cannot coexist, for perfect love drives out all fear (1 John 4:18).

TRUST IN THEIR OWN EFFORTS AND WORK ETHIC

The discipline that marks an Isaac type should not be confused with the extreme work ethic, which many idealize, that drives people to value asset acquisition over sanity, to esteem finances over family. The person who works endless hours to climb the corporate ladder and forsakes family in the process is not disciplined but greedy, not loving but fearful, demonstrating that God is not trusted as the source of provision. Rather, he or she believes results are solely tied to effort. This is not what Isaac's life teaches us. Hard work is admirable, but hard work that forgets all good work is a co-laboring with God toward his dreams for a person's life, which would never include forsaking family or health for profit or gain, is not what is required of us. As referenced earlier, Isaac named the activity of God amid his disciplined digging and re-digging of wells. If God is not discerned and named in process, if he is not relied on as source and sustainer, Isaac-type discipline has devolved into stubborn, self-serving striving, which is steeped in fear.

Discipline Becomes the Goal, Not the Pathway

Life on the shadow side of an Isaac type's discipline slides into what some might call *utilitarianism*. While not inherently evil, utilitarianism can mean a way of thinking about or doing life that values maximization of money and resources over beauty and aesthetics. This mindset always exalts function over form. We all have known people who squeeze every last drop out of every resource they have, be it someone who drives a car until the wheels fall off or the obsessive coupon-clipper who has more than enough money in the bank to take his kids to the water park, but won't because the 10-percent-off coupon to the park isn't valid until next month. The point is not that disciplined maximization of resources is bad, or that a utilitarian approach to resources is not needed at some time or another, but that when taken to the extreme, discipline becomes the goal, not the pathway toward the goal. Then all the beauty and fun is sucked out of life.

Fail to Enjoy Resources

Isaac types, aware of the financial famine that could be on the way, may conserve whatever resources are in their wells, drawing out just enough to survive but not enough to truly enjoy the fruit of their labor. They may ridicule those who spend money on an extravagant vacation or eat out at a nice restaurant. They tend to scoff at what they deem frivolous purchases—a new purse when the old one has no holes or a flat-screen television when the rabbit-eared box still gets free local stations. This miserly criticism of leisure and beauty is ultimately based not in a desire to remain financially disciplined, but in a deep-seated fear.

Growing in Financial Well-Being

EMBRACE DISCIPLINE AND MAXIMIZE YOUR MONEY

Your money type is desirable in the eyes of most onlookers. You're more gifted at making your money go further than most people are; you usually try to get the very best deal possible, and you don't waste a dime unless you've decided to relax your spending for a short period of time. This discipline, although it comes naturally to you, does not come easily. You think about money often, regularly considering how you can make the most of what you have and how to generate more money when you have a great idea or see a way to multiply your resources. Sometimes, amid all this financial thinking and planning, you'd even like a break from the weight of financial responsibility that often falls on you.

You're designed this way, to intuitively see opportunities to maximize resources, to make the most out of whatever is under your care. If you've spent much time thinking about the way you relate to money, you may even feel guilty for the amount of time you spend focusing on this area of your life. While you may need to grow in this aspect (I'll give you some suggestions in a moment), you also need to embrace this reality as one of the ways God's image is revealed in the earth—you model God's discipline. Like Isaac, you partner with God to restore and develop the resources around you. When you view yourself in this way, you come to the realization that how you focus on maximizing resources reflects God's image, the image of a God who takes events and circumstances and makes them work toward the good, getting the best result out of even the worst situations.

Rather than fighting your tendencies, you can be aware of your shadow side and embrace the fullness of who you are and how that impacts your financial thoughts, emotions, and actions. You care so much about money because you believe it's a way to bring glory to God and help other people improve their lives. This is by design, and like all things God has designed, it is good.

LAY FINANCIAL FEAR ASIDE AND
TRUST GOD'S FAITHFULNESS

Isaac types must learn to guard against and grow in relationship to their shadow side—fear. You need to journey deeper into your story and discover the moments when you decided you would always be disciplined with money. If fear is present there, lay it on the altar of that moment and realize that God truly will provide. As soon as God told Isaac to fear not, he also told Isaac (and this is the first person to whom God made this promise) he would be with him. Then Isaac built an altar.

When you realize God is with you and for you, you're able to encounter fear differently. Fear will return, but trust will echo God's promise—"I will be with you"—and then you can worship God, remembering his promises (Gen. 26:3, 24). Isaac believed God truly would bless him, and perhaps, in some small way, this altar Isaac built bookended his other altar moment when he almost lost his life. Financial fear must be laid upon the altar if Isaac types are to live financially free.

The movement from fear to trust is not a moment in time but a gradual descent into trusting in and resting on God's promises. *Rest* does not come easily for an Isaac type. If you're not careful, you think you are the reason for your successes, that your ingenuity and hard work have established your security. Isaac types—wrestling with deep concern that the future may not go as planned or that a famine in finances may last longer than one would hope—agonize over what might be coming down the line.

Doubting Thomas is often characterized as the quintessential person who lacked faith. The story can be found in John 20, where Thomas desired proof that Jesus had returned from the dead. Jesus invited Thomas to touch his wounds, and he invited him to keep moving from unbelief to belief.

The original languages do a much better job describing this interaction than some modern translations. Jesus did not offer a harsh rebuke to Thomas, but an invitation and challenge to keep moving beyond unbelief. Moving from fear to trust is a process, and it's a process all of Jesus's disciples submitted to as every one of them, including Thomas, at one point or another doubted.

Thomas had every reason to be skeptical. It wasn't common practice for a man to rise from the dead. Isaac types are much the same in their skepticism as they work hard to mitigate risks; they explore all possible options before making a decision. What they forget, because of their shadow side, is that God is nearer to them than they realize. When fear is present, it's a sure sign of an opportunity to acknowledge and abide in God's unfailing love. Certainly, this sense of God being with us can make an impact on the way we're able to relax when it comes to our finances, mixing the propensity to be disciplined with money with the hope that we're not alone. Tough financial times may come your way, but with God, you'll figure out a way to get through. Until then, and even then, be responsible with money, but trust God.

LIGHTEN UP

Embrace your inclination to maximize money, but be careful not to take yourself and your money too seriously. Plan to take your foot off the gas when it comes to making and maximizing money. You've built up so much financial momentum through your saving and investing habits that you should be able to coast for short, well-planned seasons.

Take, as an example, a family vacation. A typical Isaac type will scout out the best deals related to travel, lodging, and even amusement, looking for discount days or coupons. There comes a point when you need to stop pinching pennies and splurge on the five-dollar frozen yogurt, the overpriced parasail ride, or the twenty-dollar popcorn and drink at the theater. As the old saying goes, you truly cannot take it with you. Drink deeply in those moments when you splurge, knowing that you'll be able to get back to business when you return home. Perhaps, even then, build a little more maximum enjoyment into your money maximization, learning to be more satisfied with what you now have rather than always looking for ways to improve everything.

Check In Often with Your Money

Believe it or not, other types are generally more financially organized than you are as an Isaac type; soon you'll meet your Moses-type counterparts and discover there's a whole other level. Our little secret, as Isaac types, is that while we're very focused on making and maximizing money, not all of us spend a lot of time focusing on our budgets and overall financial situation. We can be fairly financially disorganized during busy seasons of our lives, still maximizing money, but not paying much attention to it from an organization standpoint.

We've considered the role trusting God plays in combating fear. However, a practical financial practice helps Isaac types combat fear: check your financial situation regularly. Sit down with your money on a predictable, regular basis. Review and update your budget. Check your investment accounts. Sometimes it helps just to know that everything is fine, or if you're in a season when finances are tight, it helps to know how deep the hole is so you can make a plan to climb out of it. Knowing the situation will bring ease to your mind, even if the situation is dire at the moment.

Avoiding your financial reality, whether it's brimming with overflow or the well is dry, only allows fear to further do its work and play out financial worst-case scenarios in your mind. Create a rhythm with your finances. View it like Isaac and other ancient people of faith would have viewed an altar, which marked a moment when God met them before and where God would meet them again. This financial check-in can be a worshipful, trust-filled moment. And it should certainly help you feel better about your financial situation in some small way, because at least you will know what the numbers are.

Name the Fear: An Isaac Type Embraces His Design

Benjamin started working at age ten; his parents let him get a summertime job mowing lawns in his neighborhood. As a preteen, he even landed a job helping to clean condos under adult super-vision. He told me he isn't sure where child labor laws were in his hometown as he was growing up, but nobody seemed to care and he liked to work. Nobody made him do this; he had a comfortable upbringing. As he became a teenager, Benjamin worked after school, often earning more than a hundred dollars per day from his regular wage and tips.

While some young people would spend discretionary funds on hanging out with friends (Benjamin only had to buy gas for his car), he put the money in savings—in jars on a shelf in his father's workshop, concealed by bags of old clothes. Over time, he'd amassed several thousand dollars. When he came home from work one day, finding a window to his father's workshop broken, his greatest fears were realized—all his money was gone.

Benjamin vowed that he would never lose another dime, that he'd always safeguard his money both in the way he secured it and the way he spent it. His once natural inclinations toward making money and maximizing it morphed into a fear-driven approach to never losing when it came to money. He obsessed over always finding the best deals; he always had to win, and win big, in negotiations.

When, as adults, Benjamin and I first met, he'd accumulated a massive amount of wealth. His summertime jobs had trained him to be an entrepreneur, and now he owned his own company. His challenge, however, was that while his wealth had grown, so had his fear of losing his money. He was always worried about money, and always sought to make more of it and make the most of whatever he gained. Money and fear of losing it now controlled Benjamin.

As we peeled back the layers of time from his story, we discovered the moment when he determined he'd never again be taken advantage of financially, that moment when someone stole his young life's savings. In that moment, Benjamin named his fear—he feared losing it all again. It's rare that you'll see a man like Benjamin cry, but as we sat together, he became a sixteen-year-old boy in a puddle of tears before my eyes. What was beautiful was that, in this moment, we were able to reclaim the very best of what was present as a young boy, but which was stolen from him in youth—the desire to be disciplined with money, to maximize it.

Over the coming months, as Benjamin learned more about the benefits and shadow side of his Isaac money type, he loosened the death grip he held on his money. He analyzed his financial situation and realized that off the interest alone from some of his investments, he could send under-resourced children to sports camp. He even found the space in his schedule to volunteer.

Benjamin still battles the tendency to hoard his possessions. But he's better able to name the fear, and when he sees it coming, to draw on the best of his Isaac-type tendencies and use his disciplined approach to money to fund young people's dreams.

☙ A BLESSING FOR ISAAC TYPES ☙

We see God in you when we watch you take desperate situations and turn them into something wonderful. You won't quit on us—you see the potential resident in each of us and you're committed to making the most of every moment and opportunity. You remind us that God loves and is not afraid of a good mess, because in the mess resides the potential for restoration. We're confident when you're on the scene because we know you'll steward whatever is within your care to the utmost of your ability. We rest assured that you won't quit, that you'll remain responsible. Thank you for helping us catch a glimpse of the God who makes all things new, who works toward new creation, reconciliation, and redemption, day after day.

☙ SCRIPTURES FOR THE DISCIPLINED SOUL ☙

Read the following Scriptures, each accompanied by words to personalize this exercise. Notice the one with which you most resonate. Then softly read it aloud several times, write it out, and ponder it until you can almost recall it from memory. Over the coming days, find affirmation in knowing that you bring God's love into the world in meaningful ways, and that the Scriptures affirm your way of being in the world related to resources.

- I don't have to fear the future because God's command and promise to me is "Do not be afraid, for I am with you; I will bless you" (Gen. 26:24).
- As I make the most out of what I've been given, my desire is to hear God say, "Well done, good and faithful [daughter/son]! You have been faithful with a few things; I will put you in charge of many things" (Matt. 25:21).
- God has called me, with my desire to maximize and restore resources, to be a "Restorer of Streets with Dwellings" (Isa. 58:12).

✒ REFLECTION QUESTIONS FOR ISAAC TYPES ✒

- In what ways are you disciplined with money? How does this make you feel?
- Who else in your life is an Isaac type?
- With which of the core characteristics or stories about Isaac or Isaac types did you most resonate and why? How do you see yourself in light of this characteristic or story?
- Do you experience financial tension with certain people? If so, in what way might your Isaac money type contribute to this tension?
- What is one thing you plan to do differently with money now that you understand your Isaac money type?
- What is the greatest truth you've learned about the Isaac money type?

CHAPTER 4

JACOB—BEAUTY

If I [Jacob] have found favor in your eyes, accept
this gift from me. For to see your face is like seeing
the face of God.

GEN. 33:10

When Jacob learned his brother, Esau, was plotting to kill him for tricking their father into blessing him instead of Esau—the rightful blessing recipient—Jacob fled for his life. To save Jacob's life, Rebekah, his mother, encouraged him to go to live with his uncle, Laban, until Esau's anger cooled and it was safe for him to come back home.

Alone and on the run, Jacob stopped for the night. He dropped his belongings and grabbed a rock for a pillow. When sleep came, he dreamed. A ladder reached from the earth to the heavens as angels ascended and descended, and God stood above it—the God of Abraham and the God of Isaac—promising to bless Jacob and to be with him until he returned to his homeland.

Jacob awakened, startled and afraid. He said, "Surely the LORD is in this place, and I was not aware of it" (Gen. 28:16). Early the next morning he took the rock that served as his pillow and made it into a religious pillar, pouring oil on it and calling that place Bethel, which means "house of God." In that moment he vowed that if God would be with him and sustain him, he would give him a tenth of all he had.

This place, which just moments earlier had been a wall-less, open-air hotel with a rock for a pillow, was special to Jacob because God was there. This rock was no longer an ordinary rock because it marked the spot where Jacob encountered God. It marked a moment, and just behind this rock was an experience that would be indelibly inked upon Jacob's memory, an experience that would guide him and reassure him the rest of his days.

To commemorate the moment, Jacob poured oil on the rock, staining it so all passersby, including him and his kin, would forevermore remember that something special happened there and would give God glory.

Jacob continued on his journey, and when he arrived in Paddam Aram, where Laban lived, Jacob came upon a well and some flocks of sheep. As he spoke with shepherds who gathered near the well, he inquired, "Do you know Laban?" (29:5). They responded, "We know him . . . and here comes his daughter Rachel with the sheep" (vv. 5–6).

Jacob beheld Rachel for the first time. He walked to the well, rolled away the large stone that covered it, and watered her sheep. Jacob kissed Rachel (a customary greeting) and wept aloud. To Jacob, it felt as though the stone had been rolled away from his heart, as though his soul was being watered from the well of her beauty. Fleeing from home, his heart found refuge.

Soon Jacob settled among family, working for Rachel's father. "He stayed with him a month. Then Laban said to Jacob . . . 'Tell me, what shall your wages be?' . . . Rachel was beautiful in form and appearance. Jacob loved Rachel. And he said, 'I will serve you seven years for your younger daughter Rachel.' . . . So Jacob served seven years for Rachel, and they seemed to him but a few days because of the love he had for her" (vv.14–20 ESV).[7]

Seven years passed; Jacob all the while served Laban faithfully for his daughter's hand in marriage. Then the wedding night arrived. Laban gathered all the people together and threw a celebratory feast. Whether the firelight was too dim to discern one face from another or the wedding party had celebrated a little too much, we do not know. But however it happened, Laban performed a wife swap and Jacob found himself celebrating his wedding night with Leah, Rachel's sister. In the morning, Jacob discovered Laban's trickery and confronted him.

Apparently, it was Laban's belief that the younger daughter, Rachel, should not be given in marriage before her older sister, Leah, was. (This would have been helpful information on the front end of the deal.) Nevertheless, Jacob received Leah as his wife, and after agreeing to serve another seven years for Rachel, he received her hand in marriage as well. For fourteen years Jacob served Laban for Rachel. His heart would not be denied the one he loved.

The way Jacob related to resources draws our attention to God's beautiful creation and fathomless love for us. Like God—who relentlessly pursues us with kindness and generosity, showering us with resources on one hand and disciplining us in loving ways to build character on the other—Jacob expressed his love and pursued his heart's desires with free-flowing generosity, mixed with disciplined commitment. When he discerned something or someone who was truly remarkable, beautiful beyond description, he felt compelled to engage with his resources.

Basic Belief: Money Should Be Used to Pursue Pleasurable Experiences

Jacob types represent and long for beauty. Whenever they encounter something their hearts desire, they'll get it, figuring out what it takes to acquire it, sparing no expense of time, energy, or resources in pursuit. More than any other, a Jacob type's soul yearns for the object of its affection, whether it's a physical item or experience. Jacob types do not first ask, "How much does this cost?" or "How much use can I get out of this compared to the price?" like an Isaac type would. Jacobs initially think, "This is amazing; I want it," and then they devise a plan to proceed, seeking the best deal in the process. Desire comes first, and then desire draws on discipline to acquire the object or experience.

Jacob types count the cost, but beauty comes before the bottom line. My friend Andrew is a Jacob type. He called me one afternoon at the end of the workday and asked me to meet him at his home. He asked me to take a look at a vintage bike. When he let down the tailgate of his company's truck and smiled as he pointed at a 1950s Schwinn Hornet, I knew what he wanted.

Andrew wanted me to rehab his bike, if you could call it that. Spokes waved in the wind, and the once deep-green frame and fenders with white pinstripes were rusted from front to back on much of the bike. I tried to talk him out of it. I knew what it would cost to restore this bike, and I told him I could purchase this same bike for him for probably one-third of what it would cost to restore it. He would have none of it, telling me a friend of his who owned a vineyard gave it to him, that it was the vineyard owner's childhood bike, and he wanted to ride this very bike around the vineyard and show the owner so they could enjoy it together.

Andrew's heart was set. Seven hundred dollars later, I finished acquiring new old stock and vintage used replacement parts to make the bike exactly like it was the day it rolled off the showroom floor—except its now cleaned and waxed frame still bore its vintage character. The bike was as pristine as it could be.

Andrew is not a wealthy man. Seven hundred dollars was a lot of money to spend on an old, beat-up bicycle. However, Andrew calculated the cost, knowing up front that at the end of the project he would be upside down from a value standpoint. It's improbable that he could sell this bike for seven hundred dollars. That doesn't matter to Andrew; beauty matters to Andrew. He wanted the original owner to see this restored bike and ride it around the vineyard with wide eyes like he did when he was younger—a beautiful moment, indeed. Andrew desired to use his resources to create a pleasurable, beautiful experience.

Core Characteristics of Jacob Types

SEE BEAUTY BENEATH THE SURFACE

Jacob types draw out life's full flavors in faces, places, experiences, and objects that others may overlook, helping us pay better attention and notice life in all its beauty and mystery. We see this in Jacob's life when he experienced a dramatic, life-changing encounter with God, inspiring him to memorialize that moment by pouring oil on a rock, a rock that every time he saw it, or walked by it with another person, would tell a story about God's activity.

Jacob types discern beauty all around them. They don't have to look for it—their souls' lenses filter beauty and draw it to the surface of their awareness. Jacob types, perhaps more instinctively than other types, "see God in all things, and all things in God."[8]

Pouring oil on the rock, Jacob took an average and normal item and created a meaningful moment. Jacob types have this ability to draw forth life's beauty—and God's beauty—by the way they use their resources.

In Jewish understanding, something is beautiful if it endures. Something else can be pleasing to the eye and not attain this status of true beauty, because true beauty persists and remains.[9] It is not transient and has nothing to do with the kind of beauty associated with today's commercialized pursuit of remaining youthful, fit, and attractive—none of which are inherently evil desires. True beauty is anchored in and stems from the beautiful One, the Creator God. In this way, something can be beautiful even if it's not pretty; it's beautiful because of its essence, its intent, and the way it is used. Aesthetic beauty has its place, as we will soon see, but it must have its basis in this reality to be truly beautiful.

I clearly discerned this characteristic in my daughter's life, even from an early age, as she beheld beautiful potential in an ordinary object. One morning while taking Seri to kindergarten, she broke the silence of our commute. "Daddy, I have an idea. You know that stick you carry with you on your morning runs? I want to make more of those and sell them to joggers." She had noticed that each time I left the house for an early-morning trail run, I carried a stick. It was about eighteen inches long and I had sanded it down and coated it with a clear sealant. This stick became my constant companion following several instances when I took spiderwebs to the face. I'd picked it up one morning and found it useful to hold out in front of me when I could barely see as I approached areas where spiders would string a web between trees, spanning my path with unwanted obstacles that ruined more than one otherwise serene moment.

Seri presented her business plan. "I want to collect sticks like yours, paint and decorate them, and sell them at places where joggers exercise, like parks. Then I want to use that money to send children to Camp Hope." I could barely speak—she was five years old, and in a moment had taken an idea from concept status to an executable business idea. More than that, her motive shocked me. Camp Hope is a weeklong summer camp for children in the foster care system, children who may otherwise never get to go to camp, who may never have received a proper birthday party or present.

Every weekend for months we walked trails together and collected sticks. She'd see one lying on the ground, test its virtue against her knee, and if it didn't snap, it made the cut. Then she'd peel bark from the stick, sand it down, and paint it. When I asked her how much she planned to sell them for, she said, "Three dollars, or whatever people want to give." And that became her sales pitch everywhere we went with these colorful sticks.

"Excuse me, sir. I'm selling Hope Sticks to send children in the foster care system to summer camp. Do you ever jog or go on morning walks? These are great to fend off spiderwebs and even animals that chase you. They're $3, or you can give whatever you want so these kids can go to camp."

Anyone with a pulse forked over the cash. She often garnered more than twenty dollars per stick. That summer, she paid for three students to attend summer camp because she saw beauty in something ordinary and turned it into something desirable, both with her art and her story. The real beauty, however, was not found in the glitter and designs she painted onto the sticks. It was the beauty that flowed from her heart, which transformed something ordinary into something beautiful.

When she was interviewed by a local paper, the reporter

inquired where she got the idea for Hope Sticks. She looked at him like he'd asked a silly question and nonchalantly responded, "From God." For Seri, this ability to see beauty in the ordinary came naturally because the world had not yet taught her how to overlook God's activity in, of all things, a stick. Jacob types, like Seri, see beauty beneath the surface, and they'll use resources to acquire or draw out this beauty.

Their Generosity Meets Restraint; Desire Converges with Discipline

Jacob types represent a mix of Abraham and Isaac types, with the Abraham type embodying hospitality and God's free-flowing love and the Isaac type embodying God's discipline and restraint. When Jacob saw Rachel, he fell hopelessly in love, and his heart gushed with commitments to achieve her hand in marriage; for over a decade he'd have to discipline himself to fulfill this commitment. The free-flowing generosity of Jacob's grandfather, Abraham, mingles with the never-quit grit and determination of his father, Isaac. The souls of Jacob types flow with desire, generosity, and the discipline to willfully pursue what they want, and, at their best, to restrain their energies and resources when necessary.

Jacob types' passions and compassion are focused, so when they lock eyes with something they believe will bring beauty into the world, their discipline will not let them give up. They know what they want, and they want it with all their hearts.

The merging of hospitality and free-flowing generosity with disciplined restraint in Jacob types' souls can generate great beauty in the world around them while creating incredible tension within them as they relate to money.

My friend Chris, a Jacob type, wrestles with this tension. His parents worked diligently to develop his family's vacation rental and real estate firm. His father started the company in 1982 and his mother managed the firm's assets meticulously. Over the next two decades, Ocean Reef Realty emerged as an industry leader along the gem-toned waters of Destin, Florida. Chris learned the family trade as a teen and now manages aspects of the company alongside his brother and parents.

Today, their business oversees multi-million-dollar gulf-front properties, they have assembled a first-class team, the company's value has skyrocketed, and the owner-managers of the company, along with team members, enjoy the fruits of decades of labor. For Chris, all this success did not come easily, nor does enjoying it come without inner tension. He's in his early thirties and has invested his time and energy in this company for nearly two decades. Still, he wrestles with the assets that flow through his life.

Their real estate company owns much of a small office complex, and an upstairs sector of the complex sat unused. Chris had a vision for the space—turn it into a state-of-the-art recording facility that he and his wife, Gileah, along with local musicians and those they had met around the country, could use to record while enjoying the hospitality and sheer beauty of Destin beaches.

Chris took me on a tour of the dilapidated space. As he walked the concrete slab with his hand in the air—painting a picture of a potential sound booth along this wall; mixing gear over there; an insulated, soundproof room in that corner—I could see the vision as clearly as I could feel his passion. So when he texted me a photo one evening of drywall being applied, I called to celebrate the progress with him—and encountered a conversation I didn't expect.

"Chris, this is going to be great!" I exclaimed.

He replied, "Man, it seems like I'm spending a lot of money

on this. We're doing everything just right, using nothing but the best gear. Still, it seems like a lot of money to be spending on my project."

Sure, his budget was large, but compared to the product he was going to produce, the magnificent studio he was creating, and the numbers of often under-resourced musicians who would benefit from this space, the budget seemed reasonable. Further, compared to their company's assets, the expenses were minuscule.

But I don't think spending a large amount of money bothered him. I think spending a large amount of money *on himself* bothered him. He did it, yet he wrestled with the expense. His generous and hospitable spirit, which desired to create a space for musicians to enjoy recording, conflicted with his self-discipline, which was counting the cost of renovating this incredible space. Further, typical of the Abrahamic tendencies that make up this Jacob-type mix, Chris has no problem lavishing resources on others but thinks twice before being kind to himself with money. Chris, like other Jacob types, lives in the flux and flow of disciplined hospitality, love meeting law, beauty in boundaries.

CREATE AND ARE DRAWN TO BEAUTIFUL THINGS AND EXPERIENCES

Of his twelve sons, Jacob favored Joseph, the child Rachel long anticipated in her barrenness, the child Jacob fathered in his old age. And Jacob "made him a robe of many colors" (Gen. 37:3 ESV).

As we've seen, Jacob types see beauty beneath the surface. While keeping this essence of beauty in mind, we cannot overlook that Jacob types produce, deeply appreciate, and desire aesthetic beauty, or the beauty of appearances. We saw this earlier in Jacob's life when he fell headlong in love with Rachel, whom the Scriptures describe in her beauty perhaps more than any other woman in the entire Bible.

Now we see Jacob producing a beautiful garment for his beloved son Joseph. This garment was so extravagant, and demonstrated Jacob's favor for Joseph so intensely, that it led Jacob's other sons to despise Joseph. This garment must have been incredible, visually expressing Jacob's deep affection for his son. Jacob types create or appreciate extravagant beauty, beauty that draws attention to the goodness of life, the goodness of God.

My friend Vangie tends toward the way of Jacob. Whatever Vangie does, whether it's leading worship in song, hosting people in her home, or decorating a house or church, she has a flair for extravagant and aesthetic beauty. One of her primary gifts is to take a slim decorating budget and maximize it, personifying the Isaac tendencies that make up the Jacob type, while creating amazingly beautiful, hospitable environments, reminiscent of the Abraham tendencies that flow through Jacob types. Her interior design projects bring brightness and life into a room. It's as though she sees the world differently from everyone else; she sees in full color.

This ability to cause life to brighten, flourish, and stand to attention marks a Jacob type's life, and was a hallmark of the man, Jacob, who flourished and prospered under difficult circumstances. When Jacob types entrust their lives to God, divine beauty flows through them in breathtaking ways. And whatever a Jacob type touches heightens other people's awareness of God's beautiful presence among them.

THEIR EMOTIONS STRONGLY DRIVE PURCHASES

The biblical narrator wants us to know this about Jacob right from the start: he is a deep well. Genesis 25:27 draws our attention to his contemplative nature: whereas his brother, Esau, stalked fields in search of prey, Jacob sat in his tent, a quiet boy drawn to his mother's nurture. As we follow his story, we see his contemplative, deep, emotive character manifesting in ways that remind us of God's deep, lavish, and intense love for us. However, we also witness him in deep despair, overflowing with doubt and fear. Jacob is complex, a mixed bag of intense emotions.

We watch his anxiety mount as he sleeps alone and outside in the dark. In another scene, we behold his longing for reconciliation with his brother, Esau. In yet another instance, Jacob fostered such an intense emotional attachment to his son Joseph that he personally used his resources to create him the aforementioned extravagant, multicolored coat. Later, Jacob's sons tricked him into believing Joseph was devoured by animals and dead, a deceptive plan that involved stripping Joseph of this colorful coat, dipping it in blood, and presenting it to Jacob, who tore his own garment and mourned for days. He was a wreck.

Because of these emotive, even artistic tendencies, Jacob types occasionally make purchases that are strongly driven by desire rather than rational, calculated thought. They'll use their money in ways that do not make sense to other types, especially those who view life and experiences as transactions, those who scrutinize their budgets and are obsessed with long-term planning. Jacob types tend to live more in the moment, drinking deeply from life as it is, and make it more beautiful in the process by the way they use resources.

Their money and resources follow their passions, with emotion driving financial engagement, which is a context for great beauty and also for trouble to ensue. Jacob types, bearing this characteristic, keep life interesting and generally more beautiful than it would otherwise be, but also run the risk of doing unintended financial damage, as we'll see when we turn our attention to their shadow sides.

When Jacob types find something that sparks delight, if there's any way possible, they'll get it. I've talked to numerous Jacob types who express that when they connect with an item they desire to purchase, they are overwhelmed with the sensation that they must buy it. Some may view this tendency to relate so strongly to an item or resource as self-centered or even idolatrous. Certainly, if taken to the extreme, this can be precisely the case. Most often, however, when a Jacob type encounters something that sparks delight, their reaction is a result of the beauty within their souls connecting with the beauty of God's creation or the beauty created by God's co-creators—you and I—and it creates an intense desire for an item or experience.

Have a Flair for Extravagance

While Jacob types balance free-flowing hospitality with discipline, this doesn't mean their lives are bland and boring, especially in the ways they spend money. They actually tend to use their money and resources at their disposal to create beautiful, breathtaking experiences.

Bryan, who is head of a small private school, demonstrates this tendency to use resources to elevate experiences to a whole different level. One day he and I chatted in his office. I asked him about a photo on a shelf with a group of high school students who were clearly exhausted but grinning from ear to ear as they stood shoulder to shoulder on a pier. He told me prom night at the last school where he worked had always been an opportunity for teens to find themselves in trouble. So Bryan leveraged every resource and relationship at his disposal and created the most desirable prom experience imaginable.

While he wouldn't tell students what he had planned, he piqued enough curiosity to get about a dozen or so to take him up on his offer—free of charge. They were all smiling and exhausted in the photo because Bryan had kept them up all night. He began the evening with a sunset cruise in the harbor and followed it with helicopter rides, five-star dining, and a laundry list of other mind-blowing experiences. When the students arrived at school the following Monday, those who settled for the usual shenanigans were green with envy. The next time Bryan came to them with an offer, they took him up on it.

Shadow Side: Indulgence

In the shadows, Jacob types use resources to indulge their desires and will get what they want any way they can get it. Desire to bring beauty into the world by the way they use resources can devolve into a desire to use resources to lavish beauty upon themselves. Their hospitable, others-centered perspective along with their self-discipline decline, and they bow at the altar of the Almighty Me.

Jacob is often criticized for being deceptive, manipulating situations and resources to support his own self-interest, turning financial tables in his favor, even at other people's expense. One example is how he acquired his brother's birthright. Another is when he, because of a deal he struck with Laban, manipulated the breeding practices of sheep to get them to reproduce a certain type of flock, which allowed Jacob to gain them as his possessions, instead of Laban's. The situation is complex (Gen. 30:25–43). It's clear that Esau and Jacob struck a deal, yet some propose that Jacob took advantage of the situation; the same holds true for his agreement with Laban. While it is debatable just how deceptive Jacob was being, or whether this was actually justifiable deception given the circumstances, the temptation is clear in principle amid these *gray-area* situations: when Jacob types succumb to their shadow sides, resources become a means to indulge their desires at any cost.

OVERSPENDING TO CREATE APPEARANCES

Jacob types may remind us of rock stars or celebrities. Their flair for extravagance, which we saw in Jacob's over-the-top life, and their ability to create beauty make them attractive. However, this beauty may come at an unsustainable cost. At their best, Jacob types balance the virtues of their Abraham- and Isaac-type counterparts. Sometimes, however, their free flow of generosity, whether on themselves or others, outstrips discipline and restraint.

Indulging their desires with overspending, Jacob types wrestle to figure out how tomorrow's encounter with a financial foe will be resolved—how will they pay the piper? Perhaps you know someone whose house is decorated with the latest the home furnishing stores can offer, or whose clothes always reflect the latest trends, but they have a hard time making their mortgage payments. Oh, it may not appear that they are a paycheck away from financial ruin, but appearances can be deceiving. You would be surprised at how many *wealthy* people, indulging their desire to keep up appearances, are a couple of months of income away from losing everything.

Allison presents a tragic example of self-centered financial indulgence. A sharp, well-put-together businesswoman, she's started numerous companies, and with each new venture her assets multiplied exponentially. Every time Allison experienced success, she showered herself and her friends with the overflow of her wealth. Every year she bought a new car, one of her friends received a boat, and another friend received an all-expenses-paid trip to the Caribbean, which seemed excessive because her friend lived in Florida in the first place. But that was Allison's style—wide open and free flowing with finances. Life in Allison's wake was a sea of blessing. Sometimes, however, the sea got a bit choppy.

Allison started numerous companies because she never learned to keep her lifestyle in pace with the growth of her companies; her generosity and hospitality outweighed her discipline. She leveraged every line of credit she had. When her cash outflow exceeded her income, her upkeep became her downfall. Friends and acquaintances all knew when Allison pulled into the driveway with a different, more affordable automobile and spoke of how *God had humbled her*, that times were tough. In reality, she didn't need God to bring low her companies—give her long enough and she'd do it herself. She opened and closed several limited liability companies in just a few short years.

Though Allison was always generous with her resources, regularly donating large sums to her favorite nonprofits and giving even more to her friends, her income could not keep pace with her hospitality and extravagant lifestyle, or, for that matter, her ego. Allison's shadow side cast a recurring darkness over her financial well-being.

LIVING FULL-THROTTLE, BUT EXPERIENCING EMPTINESS

We've discussed how Jacob types tend toward the dramatic, both emotionally and in how they use money. Again, this characteristic can bring beauty into the world in wonderful ways. However, in the shadows, it can also drain a Jacob type.

The Scriptures teach that those who pursue wealth do so

at risk of creating pain in their own souls (1 Tim. 6:9). In itself, money is entirely morally neutral, but also empty, and pursuing it as a source of pleasure is dangerous. Thinking that having more of it will bring satisfaction is a faulty assumption. Believing that creating beautiful experiences or surrounding ourselves with beauty will fill the longing in our souls, which is ultimately a longing for the good and beautiful God, will leave us hopelessly wanting for more—there's never enough of anything: vacations, cars, evenings on the town; you name it. We'll fill our lives with stuff and still feel hollow. Many people I know who possess the resources to surround themselves with unfathomable amounts of beauty are also the most emotionally bankrupt.

As we learned from Jacob's life, if we practice the presence of God in our resources—as he did, honoring God by pouring oil onto a rock to remind himself and others of what God had done—we'll guard against making money, or beautiful things or experiences, the source of our joy. Resources will remain a tool to bring God's beauty into the world, rather than a goal we pursue in and of itself, a form of idolatry.

Growing in Financial Well-Being

Embrace the Desire to Bring Beauty to the World

Without Jacob types, the world is just a bit drabber. You're often looked to as one who can turn an intense situation around, or perhaps come in with a fresh and innovative perspective on how to make a project, home, or situation turn toward beauty. Others may look at the way you relate to money and think you're being extravagant. This can be the case. However, it is more likely that you see the world in fuller color than the average person, whether this is through music, design, art, or even relationships—you see what something can be as opposed to what it is. You love deeply, so use your money to express that deep love for the world around you in responsible ways.

Embrace your design; claim your tendency to create beauty as a partnership with God, who makes all things beautiful in their time (Eccl. 3:11). You may have resisted your inclinations toward beauty; perhaps you've even been told people of faith should shun beauty, instead living more austere lives. We'd have to work against the whole of Scripture and the revelation of God's beauty in creation to take them seriously, so don't. Let beauty flow in and through you, for God is beautiful.

ACCEPT THAT YOU WILL WRESTLE BETWEEN HOSPITALITY AND DISCIPLINE

You'll always wrestle with the tension between hospitality and discipline—that is, the over-the-top, free-flowing generosity that brims forth from your soul and the feeling that you could be doing more with your money. This is by design, and it keeps you in balance—you embody the best of Abraham and Isaac, reconciling hospitality and discipline when it comes to money. Awareness that you'll wrestle with this tension is a first step toward becoming at peace with your financial design. Viewing this characteristic as a gift that guards you from sliding into indulgence will keep you humble, in the best of ways.

REMAIN OTHERS-MINDED

Beauty is not about you. You're here to bring God's true beauty into the world around you; the mix of hospitality and discipline is desperately needed to do so. Many cultures celebrate self-excess, seeking to make stars out of those with talent or influence. Allow the hospitality within you to continually orient you toward others, keeping you from self-indulgence and ultimately pride. It's often said we are blessed so we can be a blessing. While not speaking explicitly about finances, the principle the apostle Paul set forth applies to the way we handle money: God comforts us "so that we can comfort those in any trouble with the comfort we ourselves receive from God" (2 Cor. 1:4). At your best, this comes naturally. When your shadow side casts upon your finances, you'll lavish too much financial energy on yourself.

Build rhythms of grace into your giving that orient you toward others. Perhaps a local school needs resources, a relative has fallen on hard times, or an organization needs people to volunteer time and finances. Being a God-centered person leads you to become an others-centered person with God's beautiful love. This orientation will keep you from thinking too much of yourself and falling into pride.

PLAN FOR MOMENTS TO COME

One way to guard against your shadow side is to take a longer-term view of the consequences of your financial decisions. You'll need to make certain that, amid all the opportunities to engage with your heart's desires now, you have planned financially for what your heart will desire down the road. After taking care of key needs first (utilities, savings, groceries, and so on), have a sustainable, long-term financial plan that will allow you to be a blessing to the world for years to come. When it comes to money, you like to live in the moment, but you also need to plan for moments to come.

Embrace Financial Boundaries

Remember that boundaries make all things beautiful. The Lord set the limits between earth and sky, between sea and land. Know when enough is enough, and if you have a hard time discerning this or taking the long view, ask someone to help. It can be tough to rein in your energies, and even your money, so it's a good thing for you to have a budget set aside for projects and people you want to bless with your creative touch. Others may seek to drain the life and resources out of you, so realize there is nothing beautiful about a bloodsucker—you may have to flick them off your finances and move on. Honor your boundaries and make things beautiful in the space between them.

Keep Attention Off Yourself

Jesus taught that when you give, you should do so without letting the left hand know what your right hand is doing (Matt. 6:3). He understood the tendency of the human heart to want to take credit for doing good, or perhaps to use a financial gift as leverage for when you need to cash in a favor. Avoid this temptation at all costs. In so much as it is in your power, be generous covertly, in secret, and allow the person to wonder where the good gift came from. Ultimately, you'll be hoping all along that they suspected it was a blessing from God. That's your goal, after all—to draw attention to God's beauty.

From Shame to Delight: A Jacob Type Embraces Her Design

Deidre lowered her head and sat in silence. "I've always felt like it was a sin, the way I like nice things, how I enjoy creating beautiful spaces with furnishings, my love for jewelry and nice shoes. That might sound stupid, but I've been ashamed of it for as long as I can remember." The rest of the group sat respectfully silent. We were studying the Jacob money type together, and Deidra was experiencing a moment of awareness of how and why she thought and felt about money the way she did.

"Can you remember the first time you felt shame for loving nice things?" one of the group asked her.

"I don't remember how old I was," she responded, "but I remember being in church. The preacher told me we weren't supposed to love anything in the world, and that we should desire only heavenly things."

I've heard this faulty doctrine many times: if you love things in the world, you can't love and be devoted to God. Certainly, we can become too focused on things that don't matter eternally, but it's unbiblical and dangerous to propose that God's good earth and its resources are to be shunned and not enjoyed. That's Neoplatonic dualism, not biblical Christian or Jewish theology.

The longer we talked, and the more we explored how God used Jacob's life to reveal the truth that we can and should use resources to bring about beauty in the world, the more at ease Deidre became. The next week she entered the room wearing sparkly earrings and some really nice heels. She smiled and said, "Listen, I've spent far too long dressing down to make everyone around me happy, and I've been miserable. It's time I embraced who I am." We all smiled as we watched a dear friend shed the guilt that had plagued her for far too long. And lest you think Deidre became some self-absorbed narcissist, you'll be happy to know that the following week her company posted pictures on social media of her and her colleagues, all in ratty blue jeans, building a home for a single mother.

✒ A BLESSING FOR JACOB TYPES ✒

We see God in you—in your love for beauty, a beauty that endures. You remind us there's more to this life than simply getting stuff done. Spending time with you is refreshing. You provoke us to pause, reflect, and consider the lilies of the field. The atmospheres you create nurse our souls back to health—we feel God's beauty in the spaces and places we enjoy in your presence. Life truly is good when we're with you. Thank you for reminding us of the God who created the heavens and the earth and saw that they were good. We see God shining through your beautiful, creative presence.

✒ SCRIPTURES FOR THE BEAUTIFUL SOUL ✒

Read the following Scriptures, each accompanied by words to personalize this exercise. Notice the one with which you most resonate. Then softly read it aloud several times, write it out, and ponder it until you can almost recall it from memory. Over the coming days, find affirmation in knowing that you bring God's love into the world in meaningful ways, and that the Scriptures affirm your way of being in the world related to resources.

- I am designed to see the beauty of God all around me, for "the heavens declare the glory of God; the skies proclaim the work of his hands" (Ps.19:1).
- I am called to contemplate "whatever is true, whatever is noble, whatever is right, whatever is pure, whatever is lovely, whatever is admirable . . . anything . . . excellent or praiseworthy" (Phil. 4:8).
- My desire is to see God's beauty shine forth in the earth.

"One thing I ask from the LORD, this only do I seek: that I may dwell in the house of the LORD all the days of my life, to gaze on the beauty of the LORD and to seek him in his temple" (Ps. 27:4).

🌿 REFLECTION QUESTIONS FOR JACOB TYPES 🌿

- ✒ In what ways do you use money to create beautiful environments or experiences? How does this make you feel?
- ✒ Who else in your life is a Jacob type?
- ✒ With which of the core characteristics or stories about Jacob or Jacob types did you most resonate and why? How do you see yourself in light of this characteristic or story?
- ✒ Do you experience financial tension with certain people? If so, in what way might your Jacob money type contribute to this tension?
- ✒ What is one thing you plan to do differently with money now that you understand your Jacob money type?
- ✒ What is the greatest truth you've learned about the Jacob money type?

CHAPTER 5

JOSEPH— CONNECTION

The LORD was with Joseph so that he prospered.
GEN. 39:2

Pharaoh awakened aggravated. He could not shake his dream—seven healthy cows eaten by seven gaunt and ugly cows; seven solid and healthy ears of grain swallowed by seven thin and scorched ears of grain. This dream concealed deeper meaning, and so Pharaoh called all the magicians and wise men in Egypt to interpret the dream. But nobody could decipher its message. Remembering his prison mate who could interpret dreams, Pharaoh's cupbearer mentioned Joseph's abilities to Pharaoh. In a matter of minutes, Joseph was whisked from prison into the presence of the most powerful man in the known world for one reason—to interpret his dream.

Pharaoh said to Joseph, "I had a dream, and no one can interpret it. But I have heard it said of you that when you hear a dream you can interpret it" (Gen. 41:15). Joseph answered Pharaoh, saying, "I cannot do it . . . but God will give Pharaoh the answer he desires" (v. 16). Pharaoh recounted the dream just as it came to him and Joseph delivered the interpretation—seven years of plenty shall be followed by seven years of famine. He said to Pharaoh, "And now let Pharaoh look for a discerning and wise man and put him in charge of the land of Egypt. Let Pharaoh appoint commissioners over the land to take a fifth of the harvest of Egypt during the seven years of abundance" (vv. 33–34). Joseph had just written his job description, and Pharaoh gave him authority over all the land of Egypt.

Joseph, now thirty-nine years old, traveled through Egypt, collecting grain during seven plentiful years. He took one-fifth of the produce of all crops each year, allowing four-fifths to remain with the farmers. The 20 percent Joseph collected was stored in anticipation of the famine, which at this point existed only in the minds of Egypt's elite. To some, this must have looked like a senseless act of paranoia— why store grain in case something bad happens when clearly this is a bumper-crop year? Conversely, who cares if grain is stored when there's such abundance anyhow? Joseph collected so much produce that they stopped measuring it. Then the winds of fortune shifted.

Seven years of abundance ended, and just as Joseph foretold, seven years of famine commenced. The whole world needed food, and because of Joseph's work, there was bread in Egypt. Masses streamed in from the four corners of the earth to feed off the reserves. Joseph administrated the resources, which were the hub around which the economy revolved.

Joseph reveals to us an often-overlooked aspect of God's image—connection. The early church apostle Paul drew upon philosophers and wisdom of his day when he said that in God we live, move, and have our being—God being all in all—and that all things exist for, by, and in God (Acts 17:28; Eph. 4:6; Col. 1:16). God is the common thread by which the world is held together, the shared fabric of our existence, connecting one thing and person to another. The Jewish tradition considers Joseph to be the connector, or even the foundation for the people of Israel, the one who was able to hold things together and preserve their existence during a most trying time. Joseph connected and executed the will of the God of heaven with the practical economies of the earth below. His connections opened the door for him to be at the right place, at the right time, with the right perspective.

Basic Belief: Money Opens Doors and Makes Connections

Joseph types view their money and other resources as means to make connections. Interestingly, the name Joseph literally means "may he add," and he was always connecting one thing to another. Joseph types live in this same vein. They see the relatedness in all things. They form connections between ideas, products, processes, and relationships. They view money as a tool to build bridges between seemingly unrelated parts, creating a cohesive whole where one entity is connected to and draws strength and opportunity from another.

Joseph types view money as a means to open doors of opportunity for themselves and others. Because Joseph properly stewarded resources in Potiphar's home, in prison, and for Pharaoh, he was continually promoted and advanced in his career, even when all odds forecasted certain demise. The way he handled resources unlocked potential in his life, making way for him to become the most powerful person in the land, and also opening doors of opportunity for his family—all because of the way he held resource management in high regard, and the way he trusted and listened to God's activity in his life. For Joseph types, it's never solely about the money, but rather what the money makes possible. They're connecting the now to the not yet, and resources, properly stewarded, are skeleton keys to unlock the future.

Joseph types believe money should be used to forge and strengthen relationships, helping them make needed connections. We see in Joseph's life in Egypt that his stewardship continually afforded him access and connection to important people around him: given charge over inmates in prison; granted stewardship over Potiphar's home; anointed as second-in-command over all Egypt—all because he knew what to do with resources. Joseph types believe money should be used to initiate and strengthen relationships; they'll use resources at their disposal to gain access and opportunity to those they believe they need in their lives. They use their money to network and build relationships, and because of this, their calendars are full with lunch and coffee appointments. They're always with somebody.

Joseph types may also be connectors in a more subjective or intuitive sense—they can be uniquely discerning individuals. Joseph interpreted Pharaoh's dreams and developed and connected them to plans to manage resources in practical, savvy ways that preserved Egypt and God's people during famine (Gen. 41).

Pastor George embodies many characteristics of the Joseph type. George pastored a three-hundred-person church in a rural community. You could say he was the Andy Griffith of this town, donning a bow tie everywhere he went (the only man in the town to do so) and knowing everyone and their children by name. Each morning for over two decades, George showed up at the same corner café and sat in the same booth and ordered the same thing.

George knew everything about that little town because he made himself available; he valued relationships and viewed them as the secret to a successful career. Everyone knew George, and George knew everyone. He was, in effect, the town's mayor, although he never formally held that title.

While Pastor George was not a wealthy man, he used his pastoral salary at both the corner restaurant and in his daily dealings to forge important relational connections. When George passed away, the entire town turned out for his funeral. In a real sense, George not only pastored the local church, but also his community.

He could have saved a pile of money over the years by eating breakfast at home. However, those two decades he spent just showing up, day after day, proved to be the most important investment he'd ever make. George was a connector, and most every disposable dollar he earned was invested in developing relationships.

Like Joseph, who was gifted at managing resources in such a way he created strong relational connections in the process, Joseph types like Pastor George view money as a way to network, build and strengthen friendships, and weave a web of relationships that support both their happiness and ultimately their prosperity. Joseph types use a fair amount of their incomes, perhaps more than most, to connect and engage with people, projects, and organizations. These connections prove to be mutually beneficial.

Core Characteristics of Joseph Types

VIEW ACCESS TO RESOURCES AS A SACRED TRUST

When Joseph's brothers threw him into a pit and sold him into slavery, the slave traders re-sold him to Potiphar, who was one of

Pharaoh's Egyptian officers and captain of the guard (Gen. 37:36). Eventually, as Joseph earned trust by demonstrating responsibility and competence in managing resources, he deeply bonded with and gained favor with Potiphar, who gave him charge over everything he owned. When Joseph was in charge, Potiphar "did not concern himself with anything except the food he ate" (Gen. 39:6).

In a similar but potentially destructive situation, the same thing occurred when Joseph was falsely accused of an indecent act with Potiphar's wife and was thrown into prison: he was placed in charge of all the inmates after he showed managerial aptitude (vv. 22–23). The way Joseph managed the resources and daily goings-on in Potiphar's home opened doors for him—his competence made connections, and his connections created opportunities.

Like Joseph, Joseph types take resource management seriously, especially when the resources belong to another person. They view this as a sacred trust, which, if cared for properly, will lead to greater levels of trust being bestowed on them. Joseph always started at the bottom and worked his way up. You'll notice as you study Joseph's life that his highest rank was always second in command, and this did not seem to concern him. His primary objective was to take care of other people's resources, and the reason he was afforded this almost unmonitored access to other people's resources was because he took other people's resources as seriously as his own. He knew God would take care of the rest, even his own promotion and well-being.

HAVE THE ABILITY TO CREATE AND STREAMLINE FINANCIAL SYSTEMS

Many Joseph types are also proficient administrators who can create financial systems—they take a concept and create a plan or process that leads to success. Their mindset of connectedness helps them discern how one thing flows into and from another, how the system works and can better work. They cross-pollinate, connecting the dots between one thing and another. They'll impress you with their ability to make sense of seemingly disparate or unrelated events or pieces of information.

The way Joseph created systems to collect and ration food in Egypt illustrates this characteristic: he collected one-fifth of the crop on the front end of famine and disseminated the reserves during famine according to the people's needs, which he calculated based on the number of their dependents. Whereas an Abraham type is overflowing with hospitality and generosity, sometimes beyond what is needed, a Joseph type is systematic, giving what is necessary for others to have the opportunities they need to continue on.

The administrative acumen that comes naturally to many Joseph types ensures that order emerges from disorganization. Administration, for Joseph types, is more than simply the organization of paper clips and delivering phone messages to high-ranking executives—they may not even be detail-oriented like their Moses-type counterparts. Administration is a spiritual gift, a unique and God-given powerful ability that allows a person to clearly map the steps between what presently is and what needs to transpire. This administrative insight enables Joseph types to *work the system*, which as you'll soon discover can play into their shadow sides. Joseph types organize resources and create systems and plans that achieve desired ends. They're similar to their Isaac-type counterparts in one regard: they're gifted at creating processes that generate money and minimize waste.

Believe Helping Others Succeed Is Integral to Personal Success

A pattern emerges in Joseph's life when one reads his story cover to cover. First he's thrown into a pit and sold into slavery, but then he's at the top of the pyramid as head of household for the captain of Pharaoh's guard. Next he's falsely accused of a crime and lands in prison, but then he's put in charge of all the prisoners. Finally he's placed in charge of all of Egypt, second only to Pharaoh. Why?

Because he made the most of every opportunity, properly managing other people's resources wherever he was, and because of this, he was always trusted. His careful stewardship in helping others succeed led to his own success. He was trusted because he always sought the benefit of another and never solely his own benefit. For this reason, Joseph was continually elevated. Rising tides lift all boats, and Joseph types want others to succeed as much as they desire their own success.

A friend once gave a talk on the importance of being well connected and engaged in one's community. He told the following story, which does a great job of illustrating a Joseph type's mindset.

> There once was a farmer who grew award-winning corn. Each year he entered his corn in the state fair where it won a blue ribbon. One year a newspaper reporter interviewed him and learned something interesting about how he grew it. The reporter discovered that the farmer shared his seed corn with his neighbors. "How can you afford to share your best seed corn with your neighbors when they are entering corn in competition with yours each year?" the reporter asked. "Why sir," said the farmer, "didn't you know? The wind picks up pollen from the ripening corn and swirls it from field to field. If my neighbors grow inferior corn, cross-pollination

will steadily degrade the quality of my corn. If I am to grow good corn, I must help my neighbors grow good corn."

He is very much aware of the connectedness of life. His corn cannot improve unless his neighbor's corn also improves. So it is with our lives. Those who choose to live in peace must help their neighbors to live in peace. Those who choose to live well must help others to live well, for the value of a life is measured by the lives it touches. And those who choose to be happy must help others to find happiness, for the welfare of each is bound up with the welfare of all. The lesson for each of us is this: if we are to grow good corn, we must help our neighbors grow good corn.[10]

My friend Jay is a strong example of a Joseph type. I knew he was influential in our city, but I didn't know why. The secret to Jay's success, I discovered, was his keen ability not only to manage vast financial assets as a wealth management advisor, but also to make connections, seeking to enhance the capacity and influence of those around him.

Jay invests his time and money to support local nonprofits and developing businesses, many of which do immense good both locally and abroad to alleviate human suffering and develop leaders. He's open-handed with his money, and because of his generosity and wisdom, people invite Jay to collaborate on projects or initiatives, to sit on boards or councils. This only strengthens his network of relationships, which in turn supports his own work, ministry, and financial stability.

Jay, typical of healthy Joseph types, connects what people need with opportunities that are good for them and is not driven to help others for self-serving reasons. Henri Nouwen illustrates this principle through a few thoughts about fundraising and investing: "The point of view of the gospel says to people: 'I will take this money and invest it only if it is good for your spiritual journey, only if it is good for your spiritual health.'"[11] Joseph types begin with what is best for the other person because they know this will benefit the most people and God's kingdom over the long-term.

Jay is one of those individuals with whom you want to connect if you're in transition or seeking to gain access to key individuals who may open doors for you. Jay is sort of a gatekeeper. It seemed that every day Jay was having lunch with someone, talking about the other person's financial or career goals, or perhaps coming alongside a nonprofit or leader in our community who was planning an event that would have positive impact on our city. Certainly, wealth management advisors have lots of conversations with prospective clients; however, Jay's networking transcended anything you might expect in this regard, and his networking took him well beyond personal business opportunities.

Joseph types like Jay always just seem to show up. If there's something important brewing in an organization or out in the community, their desire to see others and the community succeed will draw Joseph types onto the scene. Joseph types often find themselves invited to join a conversation because of their ability to make things happen, and they are known as being well networked, so they're people of influence whose presence is desirable and valuable.

USE THEIR CONNECTIONS TO PROVIDE FOR OTHERS

Joseph's life created a sort of halo effect, shining light not only on his own life but also on the lives of those around him. Joseph was the connector between the twelve tribes of Israel (his brothers) and their opportunity to become a solidified people. If not for Joseph, they would have died of starvation during the famine. Joseph kept the dream alive for God's people to succeed.

We continually see Joseph providing for others, and this is a hallmark of Joseph types—they use their resources to make connections that provide for others. When sending his brothers home from Egypt, Joseph told them, "I will provide for you there, because five years of famine are still to come. Otherwise you and your household and all who belong to you will become destitute" (Gen. 45:11). Again, in Genesis 47:12, we're told, "Joseph also provided his father and his brothers and all his father's household with food, according to the number of their children."

Eventually, we see that "all the world came to Egypt to buy grain from Joseph" (41:57). Joseph became the hub around which the economy of his day revolved, and he used this influence to sustain many lives (50:20). Joseph's influence was not based in his ownership of resources but rather in his access to them. Connectivity centers on this principle: access, not necessarily ownership, is the seedbed for opportunity. Joseph types are well-connected providers; their success enables them to provide for others.

Joseph types draw on their resources, even their network of relationships, to connect those in need with opportunity. Toward the end of Joseph's narrative, the same family members who threw him into a pit and put a price tag on his head received jobs in Egypt because of Joseph's connectedness. Joseph types are resourceful people because they seem to know everyone and everything going on; their network serves as a resource pool for those who are in transition, financial distress, or seeking opportunity.

Focus Extensively on the Financial Future

Joseph caught a glimpse of his future through the lens of two stirring dreams. In one, eleven sheaves of grain bowed down to him. In another, the sun, moon, and eleven stars bowed before him. According to the dreams, Joseph's family would one day, in some form or another, bow down to him. Joseph made what appeared at first to be a youthful mistake, sharing the dreams with his family. Eventually, as the story developed, this act led to a series of events that brought about the dream's realization and his family's salvation from famine. In the short run, Joseph's sharing the dream landed him at the bottom of a waterless pit, being sold into slavery, being falsely accused of a crime, and being thrown into prison. Joseph caught what appeared to be a good run of bad luck. But looking back, we can see it all lured him toward the good things God had in store.

Joseph types are dreamers. They spend a fair amount of time imagining what their futures might entail, and this impacts their daily activities and the ways they spend their money. While some are content to make the most of life as it is and give little thought to the future, Joseph types have a pretty clear image of what they hope their lives will entail in the years to come. Joseph types, even more so than most other types, are future-oriented, acting in the present in light of their dreams for days ahead.

Always imagining what's next, Liz's husband, Rodney, came home from work one day with an announcement. "I've figured out how to purchase the Wachovia Building!" he exclaimed with full assurance.

"What?" responded his wife. She was paying bills at the kitchen table.

"The Wachovia Building."

Liz's first thought was what any coherent person might think—*He's lost his ever-loving mind*. They owned a successful small business, yet buying one of the largest and most expensive skyscrapers in the city was not exactly in the budget.

"Rodney, we can't buy the Wachovia Building! Why would you even want to do that?"

Rodney stepped back, staggering, as though she had just punched him in the ego.

"I didn't say I was going to buy the Wachovia Building. I said I figured out *how* to buy the Wachovia Building."

Liz breathed and sighed. "Oh, Rodney, you're always dreaming about something."

Liz was exactly right. Rodney was always dreaming about something. Some of his dreams actually materialized, ranging from owning nearly an entire street of rental properties to starting their own business to purchasing a farm and providing therapy animals for those with cognitive challenges. Liz loved Rodney's dreams, although sometimes the scope of these dreams was staggering, the idea of buying the Wachovia Building being a case in point. Rodney's dreams, however, had a way of coming true. He was always studying the markets, talking with experts in real estate, finance, and city planning. Rodney knew what was coming on the horizon, and more than that, he could trust his *hunches* because, generally, they were right when it came to business.

The string of rental properties they owned was often made available free of charge or at a reduced rate to ministry couples and missionaries. He never bought the Wachovia Building, but honestly, it would not have surprised me if he had. Rodney, like other Joseph types, was a dreamer, and he focused on how to enrich the lives of his family and those around him by the way he used money.

HAVE STRONG INCLINATIONS ABOUT FUTURE FINANCIAL REALITIES

Emerging from their inclinations toward the future, some Joseph types share a related, somewhat unusual characteristic: their ability to sense the "financial rains" ahead. Old men have told me they can feel the rain in their bones before the first cloud fills the sky. I've been in a boat with my grandfather when he could smell the rain coming, although I could only see fair-weather skies.

Some would say this intuition comes from the collective wisdom of their past experiences, and some would propose that some people just know what they know. Regardless, they were always right, and how they knew what they knew was always outside the realm of my awareness. I was always just happy to be out of the rain.

Here's what has always intrigued me about Joseph types, although we must be careful not to assume this is a skill somehow simply learned or that all Joseph types embody this inclination or ability: some Joseph types actually intuit events that are yet to happen. Like Joseph, who interpreted Pharaoh's dreams, claiming it was God who gave this type of insight, some Joseph types seem to have the uncanny ability to sense the rain financially before it arrives. They have "hunches" or intuitions that clue them in to what's next. And while we cannot claim Joseph types have an ability to predict markets or that they own a crystal ball that tells them precisely what's to come, I've witnessed this characteristic in Joseph types enough to realize that, more often than not, they seem to be right about what lies ahead related to their finances.

Chad had experienced this unusual characteristic. He found himself sitting back in his chair in his organization's boardroom, staring at financial charts on the walls as the CEO of the nonprofit for which he worked stood at the head of the table. The CEO was trying to persuade the board that the present upward trend in donations justified taking on additional staff to support special projects that had been delayed as the Great Recession of 2008 lingered longer than everyone had hoped it would. Now things had turned around and a financial uptick in donations ensued. The

CEO lobbied, "God is with us in this; we just need to have the faith to step out and take a chance. I know we've hit some bumps in the road financially over the past few years, but we are in better shape now. I know this is the right thing to do."

Chad could no longer contain himself. "I realize I'm the youngest person in the room, and I'm honored to be a part of the leadership of this organization. But although I can't explain how I know what I know, I'm as certain of this as anything: things will get better for a season, but then they'll get worse than they were before. Don't take on any additional staff or debt to fund these projects. We'll need the additional resources we're seeing come in now for the rough patches ahead."

You would have thought someone had just stomped the class turtle. Chad could feel emotional daggers being thrown at him from several people around the table who wanted the projects to go forward, not least of whom was the CEO. He knew what he'd done, and he knew there would be ramifications. Chad was not invited back to the next board meeting, or the one after that. He retained his job, but lost much of his political power. The tough part for him to swallow was that he was exactly right.

Over the next eighteen months, charitable donations increased and the CEO hired additional staff and funded his projects, and these new hires eventually became poster children for success. Some of these coworkers moved into many of the meetings Chad formerly attended, meetings he had been invited to because of his administrative abilities and acumen for bringing structure to a vision.

A few years later, however, the winds of financial change swept through the organization like a plague of locusts. Charitable donations plummeted. Many top donors left the organization and invested their time and resources in other causes. Nobody could figure out why this was happening. The economy seemed to be strengthening, the CEO remained the same, and new programs were introduced. However, nothing could shake the wet financial blanket that eventually extinguished many of these new programs.

Financial conditions recurred similar to those experienced by the organization in 2008. They cut budgets, benefits, and staff. Then they went through the same cuts again, and again, and again. Eventually, Chad was cut from the organization. He left saddened—the only one at the table who knew this was coming, the only one at the table who was absolutely right and completely wronged. Chad felt like Joseph, thrown into a pit by his one-time trusted friends. Perhaps, like Joseph, he revealed his insights too early; perhaps others should have listened more carefully.

Chad was not simply speculating as he sat at the boardroom table for the last time, warning the directors and CEO to be careful during this season of abundance. He later revealed that he saw this as a Joseph-type moment, where years of plenty were followed by years of famine in a financial sense. According to Chad, the nonprofit should have been saving, not increasing spending during this season. How did he know what he knew? Was it because he had seen economic cycles like this before? Was it because he could discern that donors were not actually as engaged as the CEO believed? However he did it, he sensed that change was on the horizon. The organization is still trying to recover from these lean years for which they were not financially prepared.

Shadow Side: Manipulation

A Joseph type's shadow side—manipulation—is subtle, yet powerful in potentially destructive ways if not tended. Manipulation related to resources leverages position, influence, and financial wealth to get what one wants and values results over other people's financial well-being. We see this shadow side leaking into the brilliance of Joseph's success, and if it had not been tempered, it could have been far more destructive than it was.

Resources and Connections as Power

While it was all part of Joseph's plan to cause his father and brothers to come and dwell with him in the lands of Egypt, Joseph manipulated a situation—twice—to get what he desired, using falsehood and resources as the key means to achieve his ends. On the first occasion, Joseph loaded his brothers' sacks with money—the money they had spent to buy grain in Egypt. This scenario made it appear that the money they spent on grain had made its way back into their possession. The men were deeply troubled when they discovered their sacks loaded with the money, and when they returned to see Joseph the next time, they were afraid for their lives. In this occasion, Joseph informed them it was God's provision they were experiencing and to not be afraid (Gen. 42:25; 43:23).

In another instance, Joseph planted his silver cup in Benjamin's travel sack in what appears to be a plot to get Benjamin to remain with him while the brothers returned to their father, perhaps thinking Jacob would return for Benjamin, his beloved son (44:1–2). While Joseph's overarching objectives in manipulating situations with resources appeared beneficial to his brothers' lives, it caused no small amount of unrest for his family members.

Morgan wrestles with this aspect of being a Joseph type. She's a gifted administrator who was quickly promoted to the C-suite in her company. Now that she sits in executive-level meetings, she has even greater access to relationships that bear significant importance and influence in the organization. When Morgan interacts with others across the organization, especially those who are not high up the corporate food chain, she drops names like rain to get what she wants, leveraging her relationships as power to manipulate others to act.

She'll often tell junior colleagues that she'll put in a good word for them the next time she's with a high-ranking executive. She'll regularly make passing remarks, such as, "Just the other night when I was at the game with the vice president of the company . . ." so others will know she and the vice president are now best buddies. That's a strong card to play when Morgan needs to push something through to get it done and one of her colleagues is needed to make what Morgan wants transpire. She's a name-dropper, a power player, who uses her connections to manipulate others to get what she wants, which is ultimately to continue climbing the corporate ladder and make more money. When Joseph types slide into the shadows in this way, they'll use assets at their disposal—whether human or financial capital—for their own benefit, manipulating situations for their own good.

GIVEN TO BOASTING

Boasting is a subtle attempt to manipulate others' opinions of you. While his motives appear innocent enough, Joseph gained insight into his future through two consecutive dreams I've already mentioned, then boasted about what he saw.[12]

> Joseph had a dream, and when he told it to his brothers, they hated him all the more. He said to them, "Listen to this dream I had: We were binding sheaves of grain out in the field when suddenly my sheaf rose and stood upright, while your sheaves

gathered around mine and bowed down to it." . . . And they hated him all the more because of his dream and what he had said. (Gen. 37:5–8)

We could give young Joseph a pass in this regard and chalk his boasting up to well-intended sharing of dreams. However, regardless of his motives, in reality nobody wants to hear about how we're going to be promoted above them. Well intended or not, before Joseph experienced many setbacks and heartaches, he boasted about his dreams for the future, and it cost him.

This characteristic of a tendency toward boasting is what makes Joseph types such great connectors. They have a story for everything, a way to connect the dots between others' lives and theirs. Occasionally, they'll stretch the truth a bit to make the story connect with someone in a powerful way. They're also often proud of their financial accomplishments and will let people know about it in the subtlest ways. They'll say what they need to say to find a way to impress, to build the relationship they need. Joseph types are masters at stretching the truth just a little bit, and they can master the art of humble bragging.

Growing in Financial Well-Being

EMBRACE YOUR DESIRE TO CONNECT

You spend so much energy connecting, whether with the world around you to build bridges that will support you financially when you need to cross them or to open doors of opportunity for other people. You don't always get it right from a motivation standpoint, and you may think it would be easier to withdraw and let the world figure things out on its own when you get drained. We'd all be poorer if you did this. Your ability to connect—whether relationally or with your systems-thinking mindset—helps make sense of the world around us. You're going to grow weary and tired because of the energy it takes to connect, but you must embrace the fact that God designed you in this way and figure out how to renew internally while remaining others-centered as a connector. You're in the places and relationships you're in to help hold things together and move things forward. This certainly reminds me of a quality of the Spirit—often unnoticed, yet present to bring about the good.

You tend to see financial matters, especially financial opportunities, very clearly. You instinctively know the steps necessary to move from one point to another, even if you have to draw on the advice of experts to make those steps clear in your mind. Others may not want to follow along in the process. You'll certainly have to work within the spheres of relationships you've been given, but be wary of being easily deterred from the wisdom you've developed over the years. A good plan leads to success, and you're gifted at creating plans and processes that are clear and implementable. Embrace this aspect of your unique design.

TELL THE TRUTH

There's no reason to exaggerate the truth when it comes to your finances. The Lord hates dishonest scales, but delights in accurate weights (Prov. 11:1). Let financial matters be what they are, and don't manipulate them. In other words, if you're going to talk about money, whether a financial win you've experienced, an opportunity you have, or a dream to which you aspire, tell the truth as it is. Resist the desire to manipulate other people's opinion of you just to gain access to them or favor with them. Ultimately, people will respect you more for who you are than for how much money you have or what's next on your horizon. You'll never experience financial well-being until you embrace who you are, what you have, and forgo pretending to be something you're not to impress people who will likely sniff out your boasting anyhow.

CAREFULLY CONNECT

Your connectedness creates space for you; it regularly opens the door for you to be part of important conversations. However, if you're not mindful about this characteristic, this openness to opportunity can actually overwhelm you. So you're going to have to be prayerful and selective about where you engage, especially with your money. The right opportunity at the wrong time is the wrong opportunity; you know this to be true, so make certain you're fully available and committed when you step into a potential new project or leadership role. There will never be a shortage of opportunity for you to engage, so remain prayerfully picky about where and when you sense God would have you deploy your resources. This is especially important for you because, while your desire to provide for others is a blessing to humanity, if not stewarded properly, it can lead to your financial downfall. Bring the same level of insight into your benevolence opportunities that you do to the rest of your finances. You'll feel most comfortable when you have the facts, and you'll make wise charitable decisions that bring you joy when you bring your ability to think systematically to the table.

TRUST, BUT CONFIRM YOUR INSTINCTS

You can't always explain why you know what you know when it comes to money, but this is a form of knowledge that's real and has proven a great asset to you over the years. Science may label this way of knowing *tacit* knowledge. Embrace this insight, but don't rely too heavily on it alone. Remember, there is wisdom in a multitude of counselors, and you can draw on trusted relationships to be advisors along the way (Prov. 15:22). The most financially wise people are not the ones who simply follow their gut instincts, but rather check their insights against the collective wisdom of those who have gone before them, who have expertise in an area. You'll do well to have a clear financial plan in place with an advisor who understands your instincts, instincts that may lead you to make sweeping financial decisions on what appears to others as a whim. Having this system of checks and balances in the form of wise financial counsel can spare you from making an unforced financial error.

DEVELOP THICK SKIN

Connectedness is usually perceived as an external reality—you're connected to the world around you, you're able to connect one thing with another, and so on. You're always putting yourself out there, even in a way that leaves you vulnerable at times. Combine this tendency with the fact that connectors are often charismatic and charming, causing others to doubt your sincerity and even envy you, and the result is that you're particularly susceptible to ridicule and judgment from others.

You're all over the place, all the time. Recall the continual movements and transitions in Joseph's life, and consider how your life mirrors his in this area. His was an active, externally oriented life where he opened himself up fully to the lives of those around him. Like Joseph's brothers, not everyone thinks fondly of you. Some doubt your insights and motives, believing you just want to get rich, and that's why you're always networking. Others simply envy you. You'll likely never have a shortage of skeptics and those who speak ill of you. This is to be expected. Continually check your motives, but be prepared for onlookers to doubt the purity of your desires.

Remember, Joseph's brothers sold him into slavery (Gen. 37:28). Had Joseph formed an opinion about his self-worth based on his experience in that dark pit, he would have improperly assessed his self-worth based on another person's opinion of him and of his dream. The price on his head was twenty shekels of silver. Later he oversaw all the wealth in the known world, making the price for which he was sold like pocket change compared to the amount of wealth he later had at his disposal. When people seek to shatter your dreams and even sell you out, their actions are often based on their own insecurities, not your worth. Hang on to your sense of self, your confidence in God, and your dream. Just be careful how, when, and with whom you share it.

CULTIVATE INTERNAL CONNECTEDNESS

You're well connected to the world around you, yet you also need to remain connected to the state of your own interior life. Henri Nouwen, referenced earlier, notes that if a person remains centered, like the hub of a wheel, she can touch all the spokes at once. When she finds herself too far out on the spokes and rims of life, she loses touch with the center and is not only less effective, able to touch only one spoke at a time, but loses the connectivity to her own soul and to God that she so desperately needs and cherishes.[13] Make time for yourself, and make time for God. From this place of centeredness, you'll be connected to the world around you in ways that will bring God's wholeness into the world. You'll be less likely to boast about your financial successes and dreams because you draw strength and confidence from your relationship with God, not your wealth.

Guard Your Dreams; Share Them Selectively

Joseph's half-brothers did not want to hear their sibling gloating about how his dream forecasted them bowing down to him in servitude. Their subsequent responses were rather dramatic. They ripped the colorful coat his father gave him from his body, tore it, and dipped it in animal blood so their father would assume he was dead and then threw Joseph into a pit. Soon they sold him to slave traders.

Joseph types should guard when, how, and with whom they share their dreams and successes, especially financial ones. Nothing incites envy like financial success. Slowing down, pondering a plan, and picking the right time to share a vision can go a long way in helping others to celebrate the dream or goal with you, rather than becoming envious or threatened.

It's also important for those who are close to Joseph types to listen with grace—that is, to believe the best. Boasting may be in the ear of the beholder, and while it sounds like a Joseph type is boasting, he or she may simply be excited and sharing their dreams and aspirations; Joseph types may not be able to discern how they are being perceived, and their motives may be innocent.

From Scattered to Focused: A Joseph Type Embraces His Design

Norman was clearly burned out. The knot on his tie cocked a few degrees sideways and his hair was slightly more disheveled than I was used to seeing it. Lifting his coffee mug to his mouth, he raised his eyes and said, "I just kept saying yes to everyone. Yes, I'll sit on your board. Yes, I'll be part of your planning session. Yes, I'll donate to your charity." Norman gestured toward his smartphone. "This thing, it's always blowing up with text messages and calls. I cannot keep up. I need a personal assistant just to manage my extracurricular activities."

Then he spoke straight from the heart. "I've said yes to so many people, so many financial opportunities to donate or sponsor someone or something, that I can't honestly tell you what I want anymore—I find myself living out everyone else's dreams for their nonprofit, their program or group, or whatever. I want to unplug and walk away from it all."

We must have burned through two pots of coffee as we sat at the diner that morning. And while I can't tell you we solved all Norman's problems, we definitely arrived at the core issue: seeking to connect, Joseph types can become so caught up in what's going on around them that they forget to listen to what's going on within them. They lose touch with their souls; they forsake desire for opportunity, and they end up weary, frustrated, and needing to reset.

Norman hit reset. He refused to take on any more commitments and spent the next year unplugging from connections that drained his energy and didn't align with his core passions.

For the first time in years Norman was able to answer the question, "What do you want?" When he arrived at the answer to this question, his life literally changed. He made room for what was truly important to him and his family and invested his time and money there. Now before taking on any commitments, Norman doesn't ask himself, "Is this good for my career?" but rather, "Does this bring me joy?" Even when he encounters an opportunity to invest his time and financial resources in something that brings him joy, he checks with his wife and a close friend who speaks truth into his life, guarding against connecting at risk of overextending.

❧ A Blessing for Joseph Types ❧

We see God in you when we watch you connect the dots between daily life and the divine. Your network of relationships reminds us that we're all connected, like one body with many parts, and that as we rely on one another and see the value present within each member of the body, we catch a glimpse of human potential. You lift our eyes to what is possible when you share your dreams with us. You compel us to dream alongside a God who always sees what can be amid what is, the God who remains confident in the most trying times. Thank you for spending your life forging connections that we often draw on when we need them most. You remind us of the God who is so intimately connected to every area of our lives, the One who lures all things toward good.

❧ Scriptures for the Connected Soul ❧

Read the following Scriptures, each accompanied by words to personalize this exercise. Notice the one with which you most resonate. Then softly read it aloud several times, write it out, and ponder it until you can almost recall it from memory. Over the coming days, find affirmation in knowing that you bring God's love into the world in meaningful ways, and that the Scriptures affirm your way of being in the world related to resources.

- If I boast, I will "boast in the Lord" (1 Cor. 1:31), because it is God who opens doors of opportunity.
- Jesus taught his disciples to discern and pray for the connectedness of the unseen with the seen. "Our Father in heaven, hallowed be your name, your kingdom come, your will be done, on earth as it is in heaven" (Matt. 6:9–10).

✒ God has called me to remain faithful in my stewardship, for "whoever can be trusted with very little can also be trusted with much, and whoever is dishonest with very little will also be dishonest with much" (Luke 16:10).

❧ REFLECTION QUESTIONS FOR JOSEPH TYPES ❧

✒ In what ways do you use money to make connections? How does this make you feel?

✒ Who else in your life is a Joseph type?

✒ With which of the core characteristics or stories about Joseph or Joseph types did you most resonate and why? How do you see yourself in light of this characteristic or story?

✒ Do you experience financial tension with certain people? If so, in what way might your Joseph money type contribute to this tension?

✒ What is one thing you plan to do differently with money now that you understand your Joseph money type?

✒ What is the greatest truth you've learned about the Joseph money type?

CHAPTER 6

MOSES—ENDURANCE

So now, go. I am sending you to Pharaoh to bring
my people the Israelites out of Egypt.

Ex. 3:10

The escape from Egypt nearly killed Moses and the Israelites. It did extinguish Pharaoh's army, who pursued them through the parted Red Sea before being enveloped when it closed.

Miriam, Moses's sister and an Israelite prophetess, gripped a tambourine and led the women in a chorus of praise: "Sing to the LORD, for he is highly exalted. Both horse and driver he has hurled into the sea" (Ex. 15:21). Soon the chorus ended; the timbrels' rhythmic celebratory beats silenced. The step-by-step monotony of walking out deliverance from Egypt toward the Promised Land commenced. The Israelites had just been freed from slavery, but now they faced an even greater foe—themselves.

They griped to Moses and his brother, Aaron. "If only we had died by the LORD's hand in Egypt! There we sat around pots of meat and ate all the food we wanted, but you have brought us out into this desert to starve this entire assembly to death" (16:3). Moses intuited the leadership challenge awaiting him: lack of resources could lead to defection. If the Israelites were to survive this journey and become a great people, or remain a people at all, the resource-scarcity situation needed to be addressed.

Hearing their complaining, the Lord spoke to Moses and gave him a plan that would allow the Israelites to endure, but that would also test their faith and discipline them to trust the Lord. "I will rain down bread from heaven for you. The people are to go out each day and gather enough for that day. . . . On the sixth day they are to prepare what they bring in, and that is to be twice as much as they gather on the other days" (16:4–5).

Each morning when the Israelites awakened, their response to the resource that lay on the ground before them demonstrated their attention to God's command, their obedience to the word of a new authority in their lives. As the screams of Pharaoh's officials who formerly barked orders at them drowned into the sea of their own forgetfulness, a new way of relating to resources emerged—one sustained by the rhythms of God's grace, day by day. The long walk of trusting God to provide commenced.

As the story unfolds, this type of interaction with the Lord and the people repeated itself, with Moses serving as mediator. Moses received instructions on how the people should interact with food so they could survive: implementing a systematic plan to allow them to endure; receiving the Torah at Sinai, which provided structure and order for the people's lives, especially their resources; and so on. There were laws for every imaginable resource in their lives: offer this to the Lord for this reason, offer that for another. If your bull harms your neighbor's bull, here are the necessary repayments. Every situation was spelled out for them related to how to handle resources, and Moses, along with Aaron, mediated these exchanges.

Moses was responsible for implementing the commands and processes God provided so the people could endure. *Endurance* is a key word in Moses's life—to survive four decades in the wilderness with what we come to see as a band of often hardhearted, stiff-necked followers, he'd need endurance, which was only possible with structured resources to make certain Israel's economy functioned well enough that they stayed together and kept progressing toward their collective goal: the Promised Land. Moses had to take the long view with resources if they were to survive. He needed more than a short-term fix; he needed a long-term plan, which God provided.

Moses represents the endurance of a God who will not quit on the people, who remains and walks with them through the most trying circumstances. This long walk of endurance was only possible if Moses taught the people to organize and relate to their resources in such a way that their relationship to God, and to one another, remained intact. As God endured with the people, Moses grew in his ability to endure as well, revealing the image of a God who would not leave them alone.

Basic Belief: Money Should Be Carefully Organized

Moses represents financial endurance, which requires well-ordered financial habits. We see this in his life in the way he implemented meticulous, thorough, and extremely structured systems pertaining to resources. Financial endurance doesn't happen with haphazard, disorganized financial thinking and practices. Moses types are very organized with money and love thorough, thoughtful, short- and long-term financial plans. They find a system that works and they stick with it. They come to life within structure. Moses types are steady-handed, consistent, and determined.

Moses types believe there should be a place for every dollar, and every dollar should be in its place. They'll check to make sure this is the case, and often so. Doing this provides Moses types the assurance not only that they are doing their part to provide for their needs in the most responsible way possible, but also that they have done everything within their power to prepare for financial situations that may arise in the future.

Michelle embodies these core beliefs of a Moses type. Her husband, Matt, described their relationship to my wife and me: "We met in high school, and she was the only person I'd ever known who had life goals that reached twenty years into the future. She managed her money well even then, so when we eventually married, our financial household was firmly established from day one. Michelle taught me the importance of living a well-ordered financial lifestyle, which was foreign to the way I thought about money. She was so structured, even from a young age having a budget and a financial plan. I had a system that worked for me, but it wasn't anything compared to how organized Michelle was. My methods would drive her crazy at times."

What Michelle said next revealed the inner-workings of a Moses type's core beliefs about money.

"Money, and how we use it, is spiritual," she began. "The way I relate to money affects my relationship with the Lord. I'm engrossed in thoughts about God and money all the time. On one hand, when I think about God, I often begin to think about financial resources, how to manage and order them for God's glory—I love financial structure. On the other hand, when I think about money, my thoughts go toward the Lord, and how money must be handled in a way that pleases him and matters for eternity."

Matt and Michelle's statements reveal how organized she was with money, and how she wanted to make certain the way she related to money kept the long, even eternal, view in mind. She yearns for and finds life in financial structure, which breeds financial endurance.

As we discussed how Michelle instinctively relates to finances, Matt understood why his wife thinks, feels, and acts the way she does financially. He realized that Michelle's need for financial organization was more than her being picky about money, but emerged from a deep place within her soul.

I've known Matt and Michelle for nearly a decade, and Michelle is not the type to idolize money, finding security in finances. But for her, God and money are so closely connected that her relationship with one impacts her relationship with the other. She doesn't obsess about money the way one may think. Rather, she finds security first in the Lord, and that plays out in her finances through the financial structures and order she creates. She finds safety in boundaries, and she experiences the Lord as she thinks about and relates to money within those boundaries.

Core Characteristics of Moses Types

Love Order

Moses was highly organized with resources. The books Exodus and Leviticus are stocked with examples that illustrate the plans Moses received from the Lord and had to execute, plans that called for meticulous resource management. Moses types love order, especially in their finances. They view it as the secret to longevity and long-term financial vitality. And while they think about money all the time, their well-ordered financial lifestyles provide space for them not to worry excessively about money.

Kent loves financial order like few others. He and his wife, Bonnie, are a riot to be around when talking about finances. Kent, a wealth management advisor, walks the way of Moses, while Bonnie strongly resonates with the Jacob type, beauty. One evening my wife and I hosted a group of friends, and we all started talking about how we keep track of our money. Kent pulled back the curtain on the way he and Bonnie manage their finances.

"Each morning I get up, pull out my laptop, make a pot of coffee, and check our expenses from the prior day against our budget—every day. I make certain every dollar is in its proper place. At the bottom of this spreadsheet there's a *net* number that shows me what the score is, whether we're over or under our budgeted goal, whether we stuck with the plan. I love checking my budget spreadsheet because it's like reading the news for me."

Bonnie could contain herself no longer.

"Yeah, and then he delivers the news to me each morning when I wake up—I get a full report. I mean, I'm thankful for it, you know, but I'm only half awake. Breakfast before budget is a good rule of thumb!"

I had never met someone quite as ordered as Kent. That is, until our friend Cassie, another Moses type, chimed in.

"Okay, I'm exactly the same way. I check my budget spreadsheet every morning. I hate to admit it, but while they were talking, I glanced at it on my phone." Everyone else in the room was shocked at just how financially well-organized Moses types can be. When asked whether they do this because they're worried about money, both of them responded, "No, I just want to make certain we are following the plan. I set up a plan, and then I don't have to worry about money—my plan makes it so that I don't have to worry."

Whether Moses types have millions of dollars in reserve or live paycheck to paycheck, they'll run a tight financial ship—every dollar allocated and spent on purpose and put in its place. Sure, they'll take the liberty to fudge here and there, but by and large, they have a plan and they stick to it. This sense of order allows Moses types to freestyle financially when they need to; they're not afraid to step out of bounds with their budgets because they know precisely how to balance them back again and steady the ship.

EMBRACE FINANCIAL RHYTHMS

Moses types love financial order, which leads them into financial rhythms or cycles. Their orderly tendencies make certain money is in its place, and their desire for order keeps them coming back, rhythmically, to take stock of how their orderly plan is performing. These rhythms are engrained in their behaviors, a reflexive part of their day, week, or month.

As previously noted, early in the journey the Israelites let Moses know what they thought of their new situation—they hated it and were ready to return to slavery. However, God's plan to turn their hearts was simple—rain manna from the sky and tell them how much they can gather and eat each day. God established a rhythm with these resources; Moses mediated the plan. Centuries of preaching and teaching on this story can make readers immune to the spectacle of food falling from the heavens, each day, with a prescribed gathering amount attached to it. The word *manna* literally means "What is it?" Soon enough, Israel learned what it was—an opportunity to trust God. The sound of manna falling upon the ground was the metronome, the beat or rhythm that synced Israelite hearts with God's heart—if they followed the rhythm.

The only way Moses and the people could endure wilderness wanderings was to sync with the rhythms of God's plans, odd as they must have seemed. Resources, like the lives of the people of Israel, were sustained by the word of God. God's math: gather as much as you need five days of the week, twice as much as needed one day, and none on the remaining day.

Why was it so complex? Or was it simple? Perhaps it was both, but for a trusting heart, it was quite elementary.

Moses types embrace similar financial rhythms in their lives. They enjoy going through the same routines over and over again if they are meaningful and help them achieve long-term goals. These rhythms allow them to remain well-ordered financially.

My friend Chris, a local pastor, is a good example of this. Chris's life follows predictable rhythms. He sets thirty-, sixty-, and ninety-day goals. He blocks set amounts of time on specific days of the week for specific reasons. When I inquired about his financial routines, he didn't hesitate to reveal how he ordered his financial steps.

"Honestly, my wife and I are fortunate in our financial situation because we don't have to worry about money. Still, on the first of each month, I transfer money into a specific account. She withdraws a certain amount for groceries, another amount for gas, and so on for other predictable expenses. I give myself a specific allowance each month. Then on Sunday nights, we review our finances."

Please note that this regiment came from a person who does not actually *have to worry* about his financial situation. Noticing his Moses-type tendencies, I inquired as to what time they reviewed their finances. He answered, "Between 8:30 p.m. and 9:00 p.m. every Sunday." His weekly rhythm of checking in with his finances had a specific time. I've taken a crack at that level of financial order, but honestly, it's a bit of a drag for me. Pastor Chris, however, enjoys these weekly rhythms.

VIEW SYSTEMATIC GIVING AS A SECRET TO FINANCIAL WELL-BEING

At their best, Moses types' well-ordered monthly budgets always have a place for the Lord, for charitable gifts to their places of worship. We see a litany of laws in Leviticus concerning giving to the Lord (and others), which Moses received from the Lord and implemented. While regular, worshipful gifts may be important to other types, they are especially important to a Moses type. This line in the budget controls all others for the Moses type; it is the financial skeleton key that unlocks financial well-being in a Moses type's soul.

Victoria's experience with her little girl brings this characteristic into clear view. "What about this check, Mommy?" asked her daughter, Valerie. She always sat beside her mother at the table, watching her write checks.

"This one is for the Lord, sweetheart, the one I take to church every week."

Valerie was intrigued. "Can I give it to the Lord this time?"

Victoria smiled and softly replied, "Sure you can."

Valerie stared at the check her mother let her hold the whole way to church. As they entered the building, Victoria led her to what appeared to be a mail-drop slot in the wall. Victoria grinned from ear to ear and opened the lid on the offering drop slot the church had installed to make giving accessible for those who missed the collection time during the service. Valerie peered inside, and suddenly the smile left her face.

"Mommy, I don't see the Lord in here!" she exclaimed loudly enough to draw the attention of more than one usher.

"The Lord is not in there," Victoria replied. Then she realized the theological dilemma her daughter recognized before she had. How exactly can a person explain to a five-year-old that putting a check into a mail-drop slot, which leads to a safe on the other side of the wall, is actually giving to the Lord—who is not somehow situated like a divine genie in a bottle inside the safe? Little Valerie had asked precisely the right question: Where is God in all of this?

While it will take some time for Victoria to teach Valerie that giving to one's local place of worship is an act of giving to the Lord, Moses types like Victoria make the connection clearly—they see God at work in their giving. To take this routine act of worship away from them would create immense anxiety in their souls. Just as every other aspect of their finances is ordered—letting them know all is well financially—systematic, charitable giving reminds them their trust is in God to provide. This trust is exemplified through each gift, which continues the cycle of sacred trust in their lives. To disrupt this systematic giving is to disrupt their sense of financial order.

OFTEN ACT AS FINANCIAL GUIDES

Moses was the guide who delivered God's people from the womb of Egyptian slavery, through the tenuous confines and contractions of wilderness, and to the brink of entering into the broad spaces of God's Promised Land. Moses was God's conduit, a divine mouthpiece—no prophet quite like him has ever risen (Deut. 34:10).

Times were often tense, but Moses seems to have genuinely desired that the people make it, together, as one. Moses gave speech after speech—gather this much, keep this set apart to the Lord, remember this day as holy, don't forget to gather twice as much on the sixth day—all for the purpose of helping his people endure the wilderness.

Moses types make great financial guides; you could call them financial coaches, delivering people from their present financial situations into where they hope to be. While Moses types may not have formal credentials, they're often the ones people turn to when they need to get their financial households in order. A Moses type's life reeks of order, and those who need order are drawn to Moses types to glean their wisdom. A Moses type, at her best, will gladly welcome seekers of financial wisdom. She will help them take a longer view of financial well-being, set goals for a preferred financial future, and walk with them toward that place of financial promise.

Karina embodies this characteristic. She has a clear plan for her finances, and she wants everyone around her to have a plan as well because she knows the difference it can make. Karina and her husband, Jose, spent the early part of their marriage floundering financially, living paycheck to paycheck without a real financial plan. When they had children, they realized they needed to get their act together. They learned basic financial management principles: have a budget, save for a rainy day, eradicate debt, and so on.

Over the course of a few months they purged most of their nonessentials and hosted yard sales. Instead of weeklong vacations to travel destinations, they spent time together in their hometown, creating memorable moments for their children. For a season, they lived lean, but they lived lean on purpose and with a thorough plan, which they'll tell you was the secret to their success and through which they actually found energy.

After those few months of intense financial turnaround concluded, they were free from all debt but their mortgage. So they set their sights higher, and within two years had paid off their mortgage. Now, their quick results are certainly not typical when compared to the average household, but the principles they applied to their finances are transferable—set a goal, be diligent, and keep going when it is *normal* to quit. They were models of financial endurance.

Karina and Jose's financial journey did not end when they paid off their house. Now they're building their legacy, and not simply by investing for their future. This one-time debt-ridden couple reaches out to other individuals and couples and helps them walk their own path toward financial freedom. Each week Karina, who is now a stay-at-home mother, hosts sessions for those seeking to follow her family's footsteps. She teaches them the principles her family followed. If you were to look at Karina's budget, which she keeps with her in a notebook and is happy to show you, you'll find that every area of their finances is spoken for with great intent, even *play* money.

Now that Karina and her family are on sound financial ground, having been delivered from financial bondage, she wants to deliver others as well. This is very typical among Moses types, which is why they can be labeled *financial guides*. They're often people who are walking or have walked out of financial restraint and desire to deliver others from tight financial places as well. Moses types believe what God has done with them in their financial journey is not an isolated occurrence and can be experienced by others, that the order and endurance they apply to their resources can clearly be transferred. They are ever willing to help others experience God in proper structures and rhythms of financial planning. They know what it will take to walk the long road of endurance toward a desired outcome.

DON'T WORRY MUCH ABOUT MONEY

Like Moses, who learned to trust God, the God who came through over and over again related to resources, Moses types find confidence in their own preparation and trust that God will provide when needed.

Because they are strong financial planners and well organized, Moses types tend to not worry about money too much. They have systems and structures in place to safeguard them against pitfalls. While Moses types think often and deeply about finances, they do not fearfully obsess about these matters.

Moses types are usually highly rational, not-easily-shaken individuals who are tightly wrapped when it comes to their financial thoughts and emotions. They don't allow *what if* scenarios to rattle them. They've figured out a way to structure their finances that works in their current environment, and they know they can structure them differently in the future if necessary.

Shadow Side: Impatience

A Moses type's shadow side is perhaps one of the most apparent of any we've encountered yet—impatience. Impatience is the archenemy of endurance, threatening to usurp even the best-laid, well-ordered plans. When a Moses type is on point, his or her meticulous planning, organization, and drive to endure bring a sense of stability and continuity all around. However, in the shadows, two noticeable characteristics emerge from impatience: difficulty tolerating disorganization and, by trying to move things ahead too quickly, assuming too much responsibility, which can result in workaholism or burnout.

CAN BE EXTREMELY JUDGMENTAL REGARDING HOW OTHERS HANDLE MONEY

After receiving meticulous instructions about the law to govern their lifestyles and worship, later in the journey Moses ascended Mount Sinai. God spoke to him about a surefire cure for impatience—the Sabbath, a day set aside for no work and meditation on life in light of God. Ironically, just after given this command that would set a good pace for life, Moses lost his cool and grew impatient.

When the conversation on the mountain wrapped up, God inscribed commands into two stone tablets (Ex. 31:18). Thinking that Moses had been too long on the mountain, the people impressed upon Aaron to build them a golden calf to worship as a god. Aaron collected their jewelry and fashioned an idol for them, before which they worshipped and danced.

God told Moses he needed to go down the mountain because "your people, which you brought up out of Egypt, have become corrupt" (32:7). God was ready to kill them, but Moses interceded with God over the issue and God relented. When Moses descended the mountain and saw the people engaged in frenetic dance and worship around the calf, he began to see God's point of view and seemed ready to kill them all himself.

Instead, he took the two tablets, inscribed by the finger of God, and threw them to the ground, where they shattered. Then Moses ground the golden calf into powder, strewed it upon the water, and made the people drink it. As they ingested the golden calf's remains, their bodies processed the materials. The resources, which were used to form the calf, literally became waste—a lesson in what happens to mismanaged resources.

Moses went berserk. He hated to see God's people waste their resources in worship of a false God, but he went too far in his anger. Because Moses types see such a close connection between how we handle our money and our relationship with God, wasting resources is sin—period. When people who should know better do the worst things possible with their resources, Moses types, at their worst, are quick to the draw and fire away with words and consequences. In the process, they lose some of the dignity and respect people invested in them, because they had appeared to consistently have it all together. The adage applies—*get mad, look bad.*

Moses types may have a tendency toward being judgmental, which is not necessarily a bad thing. In the shadows, however, Moses types can be overly critical of financial matters such as organizational budgets, spending practices, and the way resources are handled in general. Moses types can become too impatient when people don't follow financial rules, when they don't act according to a Moses type's desires. This impatience may be based in a strong sense of judgment, because for many Moses types, things are very clear, black and white. And when people or organizations are not as aware of how finances should be handled, this can really aggravate a Moses type.

CARE TOO MUCH, WORK TOO HARD

Moses types can assume too much responsibility for other people's actions, and especially for other people's problems. They want everything to be decent and in order, and rather than letting life run its course or people figure things out over time, Moses types impatiently rush the process. In similar fashion to the manner in which Abraham types can neglect care for themselves and those closest to them, all while caring for the needs of strangers with over-the-top hospitality, Moses types can take on themselves the world's challenges and seek to rectify them. As one Moses type remarked, "I feel like I have to dismantle all the financial land mines in the lives of those around me. I can clearly see where they're about to blow up their world financially, and I just want to point that out and help them see what's about to happen. I know how important finances are in living a truly healthy life."

We see this shadow side emerging in Moses's life. As the Israelites traveled through the wilderness, no shortage of problems and relational spats arose. Moses tried to mediate and decide how they all should be handled, providing judgments to resolve dissensions from morning until evening. In Exodus 18, Moses's father-in-law, Jethro, sat Moses down and gave him some good, old-fashioned wisdom to help mitigate his tendency to assume too much responsibility and work too hard.

He essentially told him, "Moses, you're not going to endure if you keep trying to make everything work for everyone and handle every problem they have. Your desire for order, to judge situations, is going to burn you out. Select capable individuals from among the people to handle the small problems the multitude is facing, and you handle the big issues." Clearly, Moses had been taking on too much, trying to manage it all by himself.

This aspect of Moses types' shadow side emerges when they assume too much responsibility for the challenges in the world. A Moses type wants everything to be just right, in its place, decent and in order. And not only this, but Moses types also want to be the ones to make sure this happens just as it should. Sometimes they poke their noses into other people's financial problems in unwanted ways. When they see a problem, they feel as though they just have to fix it.

This desire to take on too much responsibility can drive Moses types into workaholism. There's always something left undone, something that can be improved. Moses types, if they make everyone else's financial problems their own, may focus so much on what needs to be organized or improved that they extend their energies beyond healthy limits and find themselves depleted, emotionally or financially.

Growing in Financial Well-Being

EMBRACE YOUR DESIRE TO BRING ORDER AND ENDURE

You live a well-ordered financial life. You budget money carefully, most likely at a level other types aspire to achieve. Financial organization comes naturally to you, and it means a lot to you because you're designed to reveal what it means to live a well-ordered, enduring lifestyle, especially pertaining to finances. You mirror to the world the consistency, steadiness, and orderliness of God. Rather than viewing yourself as obsessive about money, or as caring too much about money, realize that these tendencies are possible. However, you're most likely living out the thoughts, emotions, and actions of a person who is wired for endurance, inclined toward order.

You live with a strong sense of *should*. You clearly see financial situations, especially challenges, and therefore you are a real asset to people, groups, or organizations in need of or focused on financial management. You're probably quite good at giving simple, clear, and direct guidance on how to handle money, though you may not understand economics at a macro level or have formal wealth management training. Even if you are not financially wealthy, the way you relate to your money reminds us all that thoughtful financial management is possible and should be taken seriously.

MIND YOUR OWN MONEY

Because of your desire to bring order to the world around you, and particularly to finances, you need to caution yourself against minding other people's money when not asked. Not everyone wants a tidy budget, and yet they may still operate in a manner related to finances that is perfectly healthy for them; they may even do quite well financially. While your way is the best way in your mind, there are other ways to approach finances, and each type is led by a unique desire to relate to finances in a particular manner. View yourself as a resource for those who seek guidance rather than prying in where you are not wanted or invited.

You need to guard against becoming too judgmental when how those around you handle money unnerves you. The financial coach in a Moses type's heart needs to give the players grace as they learn the fundamentals, yet enough pressure to keep them from continuing their bad habits. A good coach knows not every play is a teachable moment in a player's life; you have to select teachable moments carefully.

Jethro had good advice for Moses types like yourself when it comes to resources—choose wisely the places and problems where you will invest your energies. This will help guard against your shadow side of impatience, leading to workaholism. Don't engage with every quarrel that comes your way; don't try to solve the world's problems. You'll burn out; you'll go broke. Enough good people are around you to help. You, Moses type, need to be careful about what you take on yourself to solve. Go after the big stuff only you can handle. This does not pertain to how expensive or important a problem is, but rather how crucial it seems in your heart. If everything seems crucial, well, then go back and read Jethro's advice again.

CREATE RHYTHMS OF REST

Even though you draw energy from financial organization, as a Moses type you need to give yourself financial space. You may tend to think about money all the time, so you need to unplug from financial matters occasionally. One Moses type revealed she wished she didn't continually carry all the financial weight and responsibility of her household. And even beyond that she wished she didn't constantly think about money. In her own words, she lamented, "I can't separate myself from thinking about money. Sometimes I strive too much to keep everything in order; it really weighs on me."

The principle of Sabbath teaches Moses types like yourself that you're not in control of the world. One day a week the Lord commanded that the people of Israel had to hit pause on their work. Consider incorporating into the rhythm of your week some space, whether hours or days, where you trust the structures you have in place to the point that you can unplug from your finances—not in a way that does financial damage, but in a way that allows your soul to replenish.

EMBRACE PATIENCE

Be patient, both with yourself and others, when it comes to money. If you want to grow—and to have a sense of being at home wherever you are, even if everything is not as it should be—you need to relax, embrace people and systems where they are, and let your presence and steadiness critique what needs to change. Don't constantly shoot holes in everything and fret over what's out of order.

Moses type, lighten up! We're going to get there; it's just going to take a long time. Avoid taking everything, especially financial concerns, so seriously. Stop carrying the weight of the world on your back. Be an influence when you can, where you can, when you're welcomed to give your opinion. Challenge the process, but do so in a way that others feel loved, not threatened. Especially when it comes to money, be patient with others and with yourself. It may help you to contemplate how God has uniquely designed other types, which will foster compassion and patience.

FROM RELUCTANT TO CONFIDENT: A MOSES TYPE EMBRACES HER DESIGN

Cassie, whom you read about earlier, moved to town and knew only a couple of people in the area. In our very large church, she tried to blend in, downplaying the fact that she was a standout in her field as a banker. When I discovered that she was in the financial services sector, I invited her to coffee to hear her story. It was fairly typical compared to others I'd met with her background— she could not see how to connect her love for financial management with ministry in the local church.

So I asked her to teach a course on biblical financial management. She shirked the opportunity at first, claiming her knowledge of the Scriptures was insufficient. So we struck a deal: I would ride shotgun with her in the class, and if debates arose concerning the Scriptures and finances, she could defer to me if she felt like she was in over her head.

What transpired as she taught the course over a period of three months was one of the most remarkable transformations I have ever seen. The transformation was not from a life that was falling apart to a well-ordered life, but rather the transformation that transpires when God's Spirit awakens someone to the reality that their desires, such as the desire to bring financial order, are deeply spiritual.

Cassie had never connected those dots before. To her, her job was not evil, but it was *secular*. She didn't sing, preach, or, by her own confession, know the Scriptures that well. In her mind, she didn't have a ministry. But now you can ask the hundreds of people who have sat in her classes, who have seen Cassie give them the principles and steps necessary to become financially free, and they will tell you she is one of the most powerful ministers they know. She ministers through helping people get their financial households in order.

Cassie has a unique gift of taking complicated financial matters, breaking them down, and giving people simple steps they can take to reach their goals. Cassie resonates with the Moses type, and all she needed was an opportunity and a shift in perspective to understand that, like Moses, she can lay out the financial tracks people can follow toward their dreams, that the financial order that comes naturally to her is a coveted trait by many others. She's methodical, clear in her thinking and advice, and helps people take a long-term, enduring approach toward their financial goals, keeping God in mind all the while.

🍃 A BLESSING FOR MOSES TYPES 🍃

We see God in you—in your steadiness, routines, and well-ordered life. We feel safe and secure knowing you'll be the same tomorrow as you are today. You remind us of the God who is infinitely unpredictable beyond what we can imagine, yet somehow remains unchanged and knowable. We know God set the world to its rhythms—sun rising and setting, seasons coming and going. We catch a glimpse of God in you when we watch you work steadily toward your promised lands, as you plod on toward your dreams for the future. Your endurance inspires us to not give up, to persevere. Thank you for showing us a side of God we may often overlook because we simply take it for granted—the God who silently works within the normal, everyday processes of life to bring about stability, order, and righteousness.

❧ SCRIPTURES FOR THE ENDURING SOUL ❧

Read the following Scriptures, each accompanied by words to personalize this exercise. Notice the one with which you most resonate. Then softly read it aloud several times, write it out, and ponder it until you can almost recall it from memory. Over the coming days, find affirmation in knowing that you bring God's love into the world in meaningful ways, and that the Scriptures affirm your way of being in the world related to resources.

- I can confidently handle resources the way I'm wired. "Do not throw away your confidence; it will be richly rewarded. You need to persevere so that when you have done the will of God, you will receive what he has promised" (Heb. 10:35–36).
- When asked for my perspective, I can compassionately share what it means to me when the Bible says, "Everything should be done in a fitting and orderly way" (1 Cor. 14:40).

May I "not become weary in doing good, for at the proper time" I will "reap a harvest" if I "do not give up" (Gal. 6:9).

REFLECTION QUESTIONS FOR MOSES TYPES

How do you organize or order your finances? What routines or habits do you have in place? How does this make you feel?

Who else in your life is a Moses type?

With which of the core characteristics or stories about Moses or Moses types did you most resonate and why? How do you see yourself in light of this characteristic or story?

Do you experience financial tension with certain people? If so, in what way might your Moses money type contribute to this tension?

What is one thing you plan to do differently with money now that you understand your Moses money type?

What is the greatest truth you've learned about the Moses money type?

CHAPTER 7

AARON—HUMILITY

Whenever Aaron enters the Holy Place, he will
bear the names of the sons of Israel over his heart.
Ex. 28:29

Aaron's priestly garments received exacting attention; every color, thread, stone, measurement, shape, and other specification was scrutinized. Tailors, summoned by Moses, created attire that attracted onlookers' attention, and which reminded Aaron, every time he put it on, that his life was different from the rest. Aaron was set apart for a specific purpose, holy unto the Lord.

This sense of *being set apart* for service permeated Aaron's awareness. From the moment he met Moses, he realized his role was significant, yet also subservient—Aaron was Moses's mouthpiece; what God spoke to Moses, Aaron spoke to the people. In humility, Aaron embraced his others-centered assignment. Now he was being set apart to serve the people as priest.

None other than the Lord designed Aaron's garments for this special assignment: "You shall make a breastpiece of judgment . . .

of gold, blue and purple and scarlet yarns . . . It shall be square and doubled, a span its length and a span its breadth. You shall set in it four rows of stones" (Ex. 28:15–17 ESV). To be precise, four rows of three stones, twelve in all.

Upon each stone was engraved the family name of one of Israel's twelve tribes. "So Aaron shall bear the names of the sons of Israel in the breastpiece of judgment on his heart, when he goes into the Holy Place, to bring them to regular remembrance before the LORD" (28:29 ESV). For the rest of his days, Aaron carried the people of Israel close to his heart, and each sacrifice and offering he held in his hands symbolized reconciliation between God and humanity.

More resources flowed through Aaron's hands than any other's. When the people sinned, whether against God or another person, Aaron and his sons mediated the sacrifice, remediating offenses, settling the score. When situations called for offerings and celebration, Aaron knew the law down to the letter; he received the offerings and properly prepared and offered them.

Each tribe, every name upon every stone, had its function. But Aaron and his sons were set apart to function in the tabernacle and ultimately the temple in a specific way—they alone handled the sacrifices before the Lord; they alone kept the religious facility functioning as it should. They saw the back end of the religious system like nobody else, and their lives were on the line with each sacrifice, every offering.

The way Aaron handled resources held implications for his own life and the lives of the people of God. Therefore, Aaron handled resources with great care; to misuse or mishandle God's resources was to jeopardize his and his fellow Israelites' well-being. Aaron, more than any other of the money-type characters, understood the sanctity of resource management and related to resources with deep humility.

Aaron represents humility, which should not be misinterpreted as weakness, but as a proper assessment of one's self. The original meaning of the English word *humble* relates to the Latin word *humus*, which means "of the ground or earth."[14] Aaron embodies this definition of humility. A capable leader, he was always among the people, understanding their needs, and doing whatever it took to keep them settled and the mission moving forward. Rather than being a removed, elitist leader locked in an ivory tower, Aaron was the people's priest and lived and moved among them.

Basic Belief: Money Should Be Used to Serve Others

At their core, Aaron types believe money should be used as a means to serve others. They carry a strong sense of duty or obligation to use their resources for other people's benefit. When it comes to money, Aaron types first think of the needs of the world around them and then turn attention to their own needs. They're sacrificial with finances. In Aaron's life, we rarely if ever see him focused on his own financial needs; he simply serves the Lord and the people, and God provides for him through the people and their sacrifices and offerings.

Both Aaron and Abraham types are similar in their others-centered inclinations and actions. Their motivations differ, however. Whereas an Abraham type is primarily motivated to put others first out of a desire that another will experience joy, delight, or feel noticed through hospitality, Aaron types are inherently motivated out of a sense of duty and responsibility to provide for another person in need—it's just the right thing to do. Abraham types may use money to help others feel special and noticed; Aaron types view money as a way to make certain all is square and just, that needs are addressed. They just want things to be right, which is what we'd expect from an Aaron type whose namesake was a priest who spent his days making certain that every detail of the law was followed precisely pertaining to resources in the form of sacrifices and offerings. Certainly, the Scriptures teach that all people should provide for those in need, and any responsible person who has an inclination toward any of the money types will do so. For Aaron types, however, this inclination is a primary motivation for how they relate to money, and it stems from their basic belief that money should be used to help others.

Their others-centered orientation and basic belief about money leads Aaron types to take little thought for themselves financially. In some cases, they'd rather think about anything but money. They firmly believe God will supply their needs, so there's no use worrying about it. As with Aaron, who owned no land and devoted his days to serving others and focusing on their resources, which were brought before the Lord, Aaron types are not building their own empires. They are using their finances in a way that feels responsible to them—to serve the needs of others. This is not to claim that Aaron types will be possession-less, but to highlight their tendency to view money as a service tool.

Aaron types reveal to us the image of a God who serves the people according to their needs, who enters into the most disgusting and deplorable situations to bring about reconciliation and renewal. Aaron, like the Lord, serves the people in love and humility.

Aaron types will inspire you with their level of carefree trust, which enables them to use money in others-centered ways. Over the years, one Aaron type, Jarrett, has challenged me with the way he views money as a resource that enables him to serve other people's needs.

"I'm probably the most financially carefree twenty-two-year-old you'll meet who's not addicted to sex, drugs, and rock 'n' roll," stated my ever-poetic friend Jarrett as we sat in his dimly lit office. He continued, "I've never worried about money; I worry about relationships. When I came to faith, I went all in, so I've never been reserved concerning where I would go to share the faith I've experienced, and I've never been reserved about money."

His office reminded me of a religious man cave, poorly decorated yet representative of his deepest passions. Above his small desk hung four photos he had taken of African wildlife when he visited that continent. Opposite that wall were two African relics, somehow reminiscent of zebra heads. The photo that intrigued me most was a 5 x 7-inch portrait, bordered by a simple frame. Jarrett and two African children grinned for the camera. Jarrett pointed to the one on the left. "This one can't stay at the school I got him into; he's back on the glue."

Jarrett found this preteen boy on the streets; he'd never known a family. As far as the boy could recall, he'd grown up making his way as one of many street children in his impoverished country. Jarrett explained to me that street children are often orphans, while others run away from home, and they are everywhere in the region where Jarrett was. Being "back on the glue" meant the boy was coping with an addiction he established to fight hunger pains. For the equivalent of about eight cents in US currency, he could purchase either a piece of fruit or a hit of glue. The fruit would tide him over for a few hours; sniffing glue would subdue hunger pains for a few days. The side effect? At this pace, he'll be dead in a few years.

"The other kid here, I found him in a shanty," Jarrett said. "The whole place reeked of urine. He and his sisters hadn't eaten all day, and it was 4:00 p.m. I just got a call from him yesterday. He's still in school; he's doing fine."

Just a few months ago, Jarrett returned from this foreign trip where he partnered with a religious school that teaches English to children, especially street children. The organization is equal parts missionary agency and educational facility. For Jarrett, it's absolutely what he would devote his life to if only he had the resources. Getting there for his first trip, a four-month stay where he moved deeply into places troubled by guerilla warfare, was challenging for Jarrett.

"I've always felt called to foreign missions," he explained. "I was quite confused about why I would have an opportunity to go abroad for just four months. In my mind, I would live where I ministered on this trip for the rest of my life." The only thing that stood between Jarrett and his four-month mission was about eight thousand dollars. "I was overwhelmed by the thought of raising money," he said, wide-eyed and leaning in. "I knew somehow the money would come in, but I would receive a really large donation, and then nothing for weeks."

Jarrett still lived with family, so his overhead was minimal and matched the mere three hundred fifty dollars a month (before taxes) he earned providing afterschool care to children at a local Christian school. But he worked this simple part-time job so he could maintain an open schedule that allowed him to be engaged in ministry endeavors. He had plenty of reasons to be apprehensive about raising the funds.

His sense of others-centered humility—which drives his financial philosophy that if he has his basic needs met and can be engaged in serving others, all is well—unfolded before me over the next hour: keep bills low, make enough to go out with friends and enjoy a few cups of coffee, pizza, and a cold drink. If he had enough for those essentials, he was fine. I explained to him how that financial philosophy would drive me absolutely insane. He had taken the financial management seminars on budgeting and saving I taught and finally confessed, "Listen, the courses you taught . . . I love you, man, but that thing just isn't for me. Whatever I have today is enough; God will provide whatever I need and will send me wherever I need to go."

God did precisely that. At the Wednesday night service prior to the week Jarrett was to leave, the minister of the church told the congregation about Jarrett's pending trip and how he needed fifteen hundred dollars to wrap up the deficit to get on a plane.

"He had the number wrong," Jarrett explained. "I needed over three thousand dollars, but I didn't want to be the guy who stood up in church and corrected the minister who was making an appeal for him. I just figured God would work it out."

At the end of the service, an elderly woman approached Jarrett and said she had been saving money to give him for the end of his fundraising ventures. As the story usually goes, it was just enough to get him on the plane.

Jarrett's philosophy proved true, but it still drives this Isaac type nuts. Jarrett, an Aaron type, continually reminds me there is more than one way to experience financial well-being, and that some people thrive in their others-centered approach to finances, in being dialed in to meeting the needs of those around them by the way they handle money.

Core Characteristics of Aaron Types

INNOCENT TOWARD MONEY AND OPEN TO ADVENTURE

Some types meticulously plan their financial futures. They run analyses based on their current assets, historical financial trends, potential economic drawdowns, and other financial variables. They also know precisely, if all goes according to plan, their retirement ages. Then these types back up from there and consider how they can get to this number faster. Aaron types, on average, have no such number. They're far more innocent toward their finances. They're not performing long-range financial plans; they're taking no thought for tomorrow. Aaron types, out of a deep sense of trust in God and the world around them, focus instead on what's before them in each moment, rather than longer-term financial concerns.

Aaron's special assignment from the Lord required that he trust him as sustainer and provider, rather than heaping up resources for the future. The Lord said to Aaron, "You will have no inheritance in their land, nor will you have any share among them; I am your share and your inheritance among the Israelites" (Num. 18:20). When the people of God did finally enter their Promised Land, Aaron's kin, from the tribe of Levi, held no land inheritance. Their lives were not sustained by earth and dirt, but by God alone. Their sole purpose was to handle resources while not being handled by them, to walk the earth while not being too attached to material resources.

Aaron types follow suit—they're not building an empire; they're likely not maximizing resources; they're just doing what is before them to God's glory. They're almost taking a hands-off approach to finances, doing just enough money management to function but not paying enough attention to appear they care that much. This, for an Aaron type, is enough. Aaron types trust that the Lord will be their inheritance and portion.

If you want to lose an Aaron type's interest, start talking about long-term financial planning—their eyes may start to glaze over or roll back in their heads. It's not that they're not interested in money; it's just that they aren't concerned enough about it to consider what they'll need or do with it in twenty years. Aaron types live in the now; they don't think about their long-term financial future unless they've learned to do it as a matter of responsibility or necessity. In their perfect world, they wouldn't have to plan for their financial futures.

Aaron types' attitudes of innocence toward money may lead other types to view them as irresponsible. However, this is not necessarily the case. Money simply is not the determining factor in whether or not they do what they feel called to do. While many types will take less pay to do what they love, financial compensation is far less of a factor in an Aaron type's decision-making process than for other types. Aaron surrendered his life to the service of God and others. Imagine the person who quits a well-paying job to serve a relief organization in a third-world country—likely an Aaron type who has stepped out of the system. Aaron types would rather think about how to make an immediate impact in the world around them than plan for the long-term financial future.

I once worked with a young twentysomething man who embodies this free-spirited attitude toward finances. Zac moved to the area because he wanted to be a part of our church. With a Bible college degree, he was competent for professional ministerial work, but there was no place for him in a traditional ministerial role. The only role available to him was the second-shift custodial team supervisor position. He had an aptitude for team building, and the crew needed someone to offer that skill. So although he was offered little pay, he uprooted his family, packed the moving truck, and moved to our city. The next week he started at the church, cleaning toilets, changing lightbulbs, and leading a ragamuffin band of wrench-wielding, air conditioning–patching, contemporary Levites who kept the place clean and functioning. Duct tape and prayer held the building together; he needed to stock up on both.

The first couple of months Zac's heart seemed into the work. Then other team members discovered his musical and artistic talents. He was often asked to play electric guitar on Sundays or perhaps to design a logo for one of the ministry teams. Whereas others on the custodial team wore steel-toed leather work boots and cargo pants because of the nature of the work, Zac wore skinny jeans and sported a haircut that would make all the girls in the room jealous—the guy just looked like an artist, and he was.

Unfortunately, cleaning some four-year-old's urinary wall art from the bathroom stall was not enough to keep my artist-supervisor motivated at a visceral level. He continued to show up for work and did his very best to give a good day's labor, but we both could see the writing on the wall.

It was clear Zac was cut from a different cloth than the type needed to wipe down counters. Still, the church had no other role to offer him. So after much deliberation, he resigned. He was miserable. When asked what he was going to do now, he had no clue. To make ends meet, he booked a couple of minimal-pay music gigs in the area, sold guitar pedals online, and built coffee tables out of reclaimed wood. While this uncertainty would have unnerved others, it seemed to inspire Zac.

Zac is open to adventure. I need a five-year plan; he needs five minutes' notice. He figures everything will work out. He's not lazy; he's just not worried, and he always lands on his feet. His family is happy and whole, and his mortgage is paid up.

Now I hear he's looking to move across the country to help serve alongside his parents in a ministerial role. My hunch is that he comes from a long line of Aaron types, and the attitude of trusting the Lord and the people has been instilled in him from birth. He'll never fit into a corporate office because he wasn't designed to. He's made for the open road, cut out for adventure, and he believes whatever he has today is enough; tomorrow will take care of itself as long as he's willing to do what God puts before him.

HAVE AN AWARENESS AND CONCERN FOR INJUSTICE

Aaron types have a keen awareness of and concern for the injustices in the world around them. Consider the vast amount of sacrifices offered to the Lord through Aaron's hands—each one for a specific purpose, and most often to make right a relationship with God or another person. This awareness of injustices causes Aaron types to be particularly skeptical of the ways money can be leveraged as power—they're always looking out for the outsider.

Early-twentieth-century pastor, historian, and social reformer Walter Rauschenbusch exemplifies this characteristic. He sought to shake the church from its myopic and introverted tendency to focus on only *spiritual* matters, leaving social concerns unchecked. Rauschenbusch claimed that by day's end on Monday, whatever spiritual good had come out of Sunday's service was undone. The church's work, apart from addressing the social crisis of his day, seemed futile.

Most were satisfied to segregate religion from social concerns, thereby segregating religion from finances, except finances given in the church's offering. In Rauschenbusch's day, if a concern wasn't spiritual, it wasn't a concern about which the church should care. He sought to correct this fallacy, claiming, "Religion is the hallowing of all life, and its health-giving powers are always impaired if it is denied free access to some of the organs through which it fulfills its mission."[15] Rauschenbusch embodied the way of Aaron, using finances as a means to create a more just community.

The way Aaron types handle money is inherently spiritual, but necessarily social in its concerns and implications. To deny the free flow of one's faith access to one's finances, as Rauschenbusch so articulately noted, is to deny the healing power of the gospel its full range of motion. Religion that doesn't reach our pockets and purses is no good religion at all. And religion that's so personal that it only impacts one's heart and never one's sense of responsibility for one's neighbor is useless. It's a personal piety that knows nothing of the Scriptures, which always call us to consider how our faith is worked out in community, how our finances play out in the public square.

Nobody knew the law God gave to the people through Moses better than Aaron. It states, "If you lend money to My people, to the poor among you, you are not to act as a creditor to him; you shall not charge him interest" (Ex. 22:25 NASB). The Hebrew for "usury" or interest, as we call it, is *neshek*. If a person demanded *neshek* from another, he or she was not a fellow family member in the household of Israel—simple as that. The idea of making money off of one's own people, especially the poor, grated against the grace of God in their lives—a God who freely rained manna from the sky each day. To demand something back as repayment beyond what was loaned, when each person depended on God for daily bread, demonstrated a rather short memory of what God had done to provide, or at the worst, a lack of appreciation.

Aaron types, in humility, remember that God has provided for them, and therefore believe resources should not be used as a means to exploit others. While some debate whether it's appropriate to demand interest for a loan given to another person, the point is clear for the people of Israel in the moment this law was given: the goal with money is not to get a leg up on your brothers and sisters. Use what you have so everyone can make the journey, rather than exploiting or neglecting those in need.

COMPELLED TO "DO SOMETHING"

For Aaron, the way resources should be used in worship of God and in service to others was spelled out plainly in the law; a strong sense of social responsibility with resources remained in clear view for the priests. Laws like ones that commanded farmers to leave corners of their fields and parts of their vineyards accessible to the poor instilled in Aaron an eye toward *the other*, the one who would otherwise go without (Lev. 19:9). Likewise, when Aaron types feel they should give something or do something to help another person, they won't be able to sleep until all is accomplished. If they don't act, they'll live with such guilt that they won't make the same mistake again. While any type can certainly be led by the Lord to give, Aaron types are motivated by a compelling urge that makes them feel as though they *must* give, or they *ought* to do something.

Kristen, an Aaron type, received notification at her office that a single mother was in need of a mattress. Her home was mold-infested, forcing her to get rid of almost every piece of fabric-based furniture she owned because it was causing allergic reactions. Kristen didn't have a spare mattress, and more than that she didn't have the resources at the time to buy the woman a mattress. So she prayed.

Kristen recounted her story as tears dripped off her face. "I begged God to do something. I felt helpless, and I knew the only thing I could do was pray. Her needs so gripped my heart that I cried out to God in prayer over and over again. I knew I must do something, but I felt like I had nothing to contribute."

As she left her apartment complex for work the next morning, she glanced by the Dumpster, and there, in a sealed package, was a brand-new mattress. Kristen was floored by God's provision, by God answering her prayer in such a specific way. She rallied some friends, loaded the mattress on a vehicle, and delivered it to the home. When they arrived, she discovered another problem—the mother and daughter would have to sleep together unless they got another mattress. Kristen prayed again, and honest to God, the next morning another mattress, in like-new condition, had been placed by the Dumpster. Kristen and her friends delivered the second mattress that afternoon.

Depending on where you stand in your belief system, you can view this as a miracle, God's providence, or random chance. Regardless, what we should notice here is the way an Aaron type's heart goes out to those in need. Kristen felt personally responsible to provide, even though she didn't have access to financial resources to remedy the problem or meet the need. This is typical of Aaron types.

Prioritize Meeting Human Need over Accumulating Wealth

While Moses is remembered as being from above, because of his high rank in Egypt before the exodus, and because he scaled

Mount Sinai and met with the Lord there and received the Torah, Aaron is recalled as being from below, a person who was rooted in the daily lives and activities of the people. When Moses ascended Sinai, Aaron stayed with the Israelites.[16] We get the sense that Aaron was not seeking to scale a ladder to success or a mountain to the heavens.

My brother, Christopher, and his wife, Kelly, remind me very much of some of Aaron's most admirable qualities, and specifically the characteristic of prioritizing human need over accumulating wealth. Early in their marriage, they learned they couldn't conceive children, which came as heartbreaking news for a couple who dreamed of raising a small village of little ones. Our family grieved this news with them as they considered their options. Soon they became foster parents, welcoming little ones into their home, even if only temporarily. As children transitioned through their household, they decided adoption would be the best course of action for their circumstances.

We were delighted when, after many months of waiting, one failed adoption, and countless thousands of dollars spent (an enormous expense for these two young public school educators), we received the call that they had been matched with a baby boy. Because one adoption had already failed, we all prepared our hearts for the worst, while hoping for the best. Kelly and Christopher, however, began preparing their home.

On the day they received official news that the adoption would go through, they prepared to paint what would become the baby's nursery. Kelly, realizing that she wasn't feeling quite herself, checked the calendar, did the math, and determined that she was abnormally *late*. Just to rule out the "impossible," because she was about to breathe in paint fumes for hours, she bought a pregnancy test. You know how the rest of the story goes—on the exact day the adoption became official, this young couple, who were definitively told they could not conceive children, discovered they were pregnant. That year, Kelly found herself in the *delightful* position of both mothering one newborn and giving birth to another.

Christopher and Kelly, who both strongly resonate with the Aaron type, decided Kelly staying home to care for these two infants would take priority over her continuing to teach—a difficult financial decision given the wage public school educators like Christopher earn, especially early in their careers. Nevertheless, they made it work. Christopher picked up summer jobs and tutored students to generate additional income, while Kelly stayed at home with their children and volunteered for a nonprofit that addresses challenges related to adoption.

They weren't done. They went on to adopt a second baby and conceive another, bringing the total to four children (and counting, if you ask me). Financially, this makes no sense at all. Adoption is expensive, and doubtless they have spent dozens of thousands of dollars that could have been saved, invested, or spent on trips and conveniences. Raising what is close to becoming enough children to man a basketball team is expensive.

Christopher and Kelly, however, couldn't care less about the expense. They're deeply concerned about issues related to foster care and adoption, and they pour their energies, and especially their financial resources, into making whatever impact they can so others are afforded opportunities they otherwise would not experience. Classic Aaron types, while they are competent and responsible with their money, they experience great joy in making extreme personal financial sacrifices for the benefit of others, especially if the cause addresses issues of injustice and human distress.

Thus, it was no surprise to anyone when they decided their first adopted baby's middle name would be *Justice*.

Shadow Side: Instability

Aaron types inspire us with their sacrificial attitudes of innocence toward finances, which enables them to be others-centered and to use money to meet human needs. Sometimes, however, taking too much of a hands-off approach to money, or being so inclined to see and support the needs of others, causes their lives to be financially unstable. As with all shadow sides, there's a fine line to walk between what is most beautiful and most dangerous about a money type.

Too Easily Persuaded by What Others Want

One epic moment in Aaron's life typifies this aspect of instability with resources more than any other, and it was a moment that humbled him to his core. Moses, who ascended Mount Sinai to receive the commands of God, was gone a long time, and the people grew restless in his absence. Because of the display of thunder, lightning, thick clouds, and horrific sounds shrouding the mountain, people wondered if he had taken his own exodus from the human race.

So they pleaded with Aaron, who was next in command. "Come, make us gods who will go before us. As for this fellow Moses who brought us up out of Egypt, we don't know what has happened to him" (Ex. 32:1).

Persuaded as the people pressed in on him, wanting to give them what they wanted to alleviate the stress of the moment, Aaron hatched a plan. He told the people to take off their gold; it was god-making time. All the collected gold was melted and Aaron fashioned it into a calf's shape. The people declared, "These are your gods, Israel, who brought you up out of Egypt" (v. 4).

When he saw the people's response, Aaron built an altar before the god. Having performed signs and wonders before, he now performed his first priestly act. Little did he know Moses was still alive and well upon the mountain, and had just received instructions that Aaron was to be the people's priest, bearing their burdens before the Lord. Aaron, soon enough, would get his job description—that is, if God or Moses didn't kill him first.

Moses heard and saw things from that lofty perch no human had ever experienced. Line by line, God spelled out for him how the people were to behave, all while they were misbehaving at the mountain's base. God instructed Moses to hurry up and get down there, and rightfully so—the whole show was about to fall apart. And Aaron, who would become the primary priestly mediator between God and humanity, was smack in the middle of hosting an idol-making pottery class, hoping his constituents wouldn't defect. God's thoughts descended the mountain with Moses as a restless people's cries ascended. When he realized what had happened, Moses went into a fit of rage and shattered the divinely inscribed twin tablets.

Aaron's humility gave way to instability, acquiescing to the ill-advised desires of others, and he found himself knee-deep in guilt. When Aaron met his brother, he implored, "They said to me, 'Make us gods' . . . I threw [the gold] into the fire, and out came this calf" (vv. 23–24). Hard-pressed on every side by people who wanted him to produce a god they could control, one safer and more tangible than the One performing a heavenly light show on the mountain, Aaron had made something happen. Out popped a calf, and the rest is history—a history indelibly inked on Aaron's psyche.

As it turns out, some moments that haunt a person the most are the ones that save their souls. This one molded Aaron's character like Aaron molded gold into a god. Lesson learned: God is holy, and resources should be wholly devoted to the Lord. The rest of his days, Aaron walked with humility and solid character, embodying the essence of an others-centered person, who maintained dignity and responsibility related to resources and guarded against being too easily persuaded by the misguided motives of other people.

MAY EMBRACE ADVENTURE AT THE EXPENSE OF STABILITY

Aaron types' open-road-minded drive for adventure can cause them to forgo putting down roots and grounding themselves in one place. They may be so unplugged from the idea of laying a solid foundation for their financial futures that they're not concerned about developing a career, funding their retirement, or owning a home in one area. Aaron lived in a context where he was supported by the sacrificial system he mediated. This was, however, his career—and he stuck with it. Some Aaron types take the best qualities we see in Aaron—that lack of worrying obsessively over finances or being very open to go anywhere and serve God in any way—too far. They've overlooked the reality that God was leading the people to a land where they could plant themselves, a land of promise.

Rooting yourself too deeply in one place has its pitfalls. But rolling about the country like a tumbleweed can prohibit you from making needed connections and building the career necessary to lay a solid financial foundation. This often results in having to

174 of THE SEVEN MONEY TYPES

occasionally depend on friends or family to bail you out financially. Stability is not the enemy of adventure, but rather can become its platform; the two are not opposing forces, but can support and strengthen each other.

Growing in Financial Well-Being

EMBRACE THE INCLINATION TO USE MONEY TO SERVE OTHERS

The way your life is oriented toward meeting the needs of others with your money is simultaneously inspiring and challenging to other types. Your financial habits cause some of us to wonder how you survive while being so sacrificial in your approach to finances. However, the way you handle money pricks our hearts as we're reminded that money is not the source and sustainer of our lives and joy. We look up to you in this regard; you should embrace your desire to serve others with money. The way you use money brings great hope into the lives of those who most need it. You reveal to us the image of God, who knows our every need long before it crosses our lips in prayer and desires to meet these needs. As God provides for us, we're reminded that he is very near to us. Your provision in the world around you has the same effect.

DISCERN PERCEIVED NEEDS FROM ACTUAL NEEDS

The most memorable moment in Aaron's life is the aforementioned one where he and Moses met in the middle as Moses descended the mountain with the law and Aaron was leading a worship service for a phony calf-god he concocted to keep the people together. Fire from the mountain cast light on Aaron's calf and illustrates his shadow side: Aaron so deeply cared for the needs of others that his compassion trumped better judgment, causing him to use resources in emotional, yet ultimately unstable ways. And the resources were wasted. You can guard against this aspect of your shadow side by not letting perceived needs become confused with actual needs.

On the surface, who would argue with using resources to serve others as a value? Concern for other people's needs should be a concern of everyone's, especially people of faith. However, giving people what they want rather than what they need may do more harm than good.

The question is, how do we know what people really need? There's no way to provide a contingency list outlining the if-then scenarios where a person should respond to a need in a certain way. To answer this question, you would do well to consider this: What do the Scriptures teach about the need presenting itself? How will my engagement with this need lead to longer-term solutions? Am I only prolonging the real issues by covering a short-term need? What will happen if I don't engage with this immediate and apparent need? Who knows more about this situation and can coach me on how to best provide financial (or another type of) relief?

Usually, just responding to the need does more good than harm, but in Aaron's moment with the golden calf, we see that is not always the case. You may carry the people in your life so closely to your heart that knowing what can be done versus what should be done to provide charity or relief can be a real struggle. Having some general rules of thumb pertaining to a spontaneous giving limit goes a long way in keeping you from overgiving every time a charitable need is presented. Aaron matured in this respect. He learned the law regulations better than anyone else, and after the golden-calf incident, we don't see Aaron getting tripped up over how to respond to needs. He had boundaries in place. There's no need to send yourself into debt to make sure all the people you care about have everything they need.

DRAW UPON THE STRENGTHS OF ISAAC AND MOSES TYPES

You will do well to draw on your Isaac- and Moses-type counterparts, those who think about maximizing resources and planning for the future. While these types can suck the life out of you because of their intense attention paid to money matters, they'll also be helpful to shore up your tendency to not plan for the future, to not think about how to manage resources in a way that makes the most of what you possess. At their best, they're not looking to diminish the innocence or free spirit so admirable in many Aaron types, but rather to help them take a little longer and deeper view of their resources so they are better prepared for life's storms and future opportunities.

In a perfect world, perhaps you would do just enough money management to get by, but failure to financially plan for the future is not a badge of honor that demonstrates trust in God. While well-meaning in your innocence, you can slide toward financial irresponsibility, and ultimately become a financial burden on other types. Why should lack of planning on your part become a financial burden for someone else? How is this action serving others?

If you wrestle with your shadow side, you must intentionally think and talk about money with those who are gifted at financial planning. Overcome any inhibitions and skepticism about finances and find a trusted financial partner who understands your instincts and inclinations toward money, can see your shadow side clearly, and will offer advice that will support you while not diminishing the amazing gifts you bring to the world.

We need Aaron types like you to remind us that God provides, that money is meant to serve human needs, and that life is about more than well-ordered financial plans. Just as Moses needed Aaron, so also Aaron types need Moses types and Isaac types in their lives—those who take the long view with a systematic financial approach from which Aaron types can benefit.

BECOME SKEPTICAL OF YOUR CYNICISM TOWARD MONEY

As an Aaron type, you may be cynical toward those who are wealthy or organizations with tremendous assets—and you should be, to a point. Remember, however, that money is morally neutral; it's how we relate to it and use it that determines whether our experience of money is healthy or unhealthy, whether it is used in redemptive or destructive ways. To grow in financial well-being, you'll need to view money as a means to unleash your deepest passions on the world around you. When you do, money becomes a valuable tool rather than a necessary evil. Become curious about how to further develop your finances so you can do more of what you sense God calling you to do.

Just as you may be skeptical toward wealth, you also need to be skeptical of poverty doctrines. Aaron types make for some of the most notable voices of our time, those who call for full financial abandon, those who take the words of Jesus in Scripture quite literally when he said to one wealthy elite, "Sell everything you have and give to the poor" (Luke 18:22). Other types, and even Aaron types, are made to feel guilty if they have any significant level of possessions. Whereas some types, in their shadow sides, obsess over money and seek to amass great sums of it, Aaron types may slide toward the other end of the spectrum and obsess over *not* having too many possessions.

Saint Francis is an example of extreme financial skepticism. In the thirteenth-century mind of Saint Francis of Assisi and his followers, possessions were a barrier between God and man.[17] Son of a wealthy cloth merchant, Francis spent his early days using his access to financial abundance on revelry and wildness, carousing in comfort and lavishing material wealth on personal comfort. Upon encountering beggars in Rome, and experiencing an ongoing personal sense of enlightenment, Francis eventually denounced his wealth. He called his emerging band of followers to do the same, while criticizing the religious establishment for its vast resources and lack of concern for the poor. This denunciation of wealth created no small amount of friction between Francis and his father, and doubtless the same level of anxiety in his own soul as he wrestled with his elite status in light of the world's problems.

This wrestling is precisely where spiritual growth takes place. Some side with where Francis ended up in his position on wealth—give it all away—while others swing to the other end of the pendulum and affirm that sons and daughters of God have a divine right to wealth. Both use the Scriptures to back their opinions. Both are right and both are wrong, depending on whom you ask. In my experience with extreme Aaron types, they can be evangelistic about their skepticism over material wealth, and sometimes attempt to make others who take a divergent viewpoint feel guilty over anything they own. What we can learn here is that there is always room to grow, whichever side you find yourself on.

Anything that brings shame and guilt into your world needs closer examination before you assume it is godly conviction. Embrace your sense of adventure and open-handedness with finances, not because you must, but because it is your joy. Balance this desire with a stewardship that welcomes money into your world as a tool to do God's will, rather than a necessary evil.

FROM GUILTY-GIVING TO LIFE-GIVING: AN AARON TYPE EMBRACES HER DESIGN

It all started with dog commercials, the ones with melodramatic music accompanying puppy-dog eyes and a call to action: give now to support abandoned and abused dogs. Stella called in, gave her credit card number, and then received a packet in the mail, which thanked her for the donation and invited her to make a monthly pledge to support even more animals. The opportunity was too much for this Aaron type to resist.

Then came appeals at church for clean water wells in emerging nations; these especially tugged at her heart. There was also the annual opportunity to support the children's ministry trip to the zoo—these babies need to see gorillas, after all. Feeling guilty if she didn't support each one, Stella continued to rack up charitable donation receipts and pledge cards. Before long, she was paying off pledges with credit cards, but in her mind, she was doing it all for the right reason. A strange amalgamation of pleasure and guilt accompanied each appeal and subsequent pledge or gift. Stella felt she had to give if she was going to be a good person. More than that, she loved to give to these types of causes that met needs and made a real difference in people's—or pets'—lives.

You can spend your money on worse things. Who would argue with supporting clean water wells and puppies? It wasn't the effect her money was having on the world around her that alarmed Stella's close friend Mary; it was the effect it was having on Stella's financial stability. Mary strongly identified with the Moses type, and after becoming aware of Stella's increasingly frequent financial engagement with charities to the point that she was paying off pledges by racking up credit card debt, Mary lovingly offered to provide a plan to turn her friend in a more financially healthy direction.

Mary helped Stella understand that plunging herself into a financial deficit so other people (or pets) could climb out of their own financial pits was just trading one problem for another. As an Aaron type, Stella was quick to sacrifice her own financial well-being if it meant others received what they needed. Mary could see the situation more clearly, and she proposed a simple plan to help Stella stop the financial bleeding and return to a place where she could support charities in a way that brought her joy while not inching her toward bankruptcy. The plan was simple: refuse any future charitable appeals, pay off current debt in six months, and then select no more than two charities to support that did not exceed one hundred dollars per month in total—the amount Mary and Stella discerned Stella could comfortably afford.

Stella still wrestled with the guilt of not giving to every appeal, but she also began to enjoy the sense of confidence that she could now support charities without leaving her own financial needs unmet. She's beginning to embrace the boundaries her Moses type friend helped her set, and trusting that others like her will step up to the call to respond to valid needs in the world. She's learned to find joy in giving to the causes she can responsibly support. This shift in thinking is a significant movement toward freedom in Stella's heart, one that is helping her grow in her own ability to trust that God desires to meet needs even more than she does, and he will draw on others to do precisely this.

❧ A BLESSING FOR AARON TYPES ❧

We see God in you—in your unfailing devotion to love, serve, and support those often underserved or overlooked. You always show up when we need you. Sometimes we take advantage of you, much like we take for granted God's goodness in our lives. But we see you more clearly now, and we love you. Your humility reminds us of the God who loves us amid all our hang-ups and setbacks, who desires to gather us close like a hen gathers her chicks under her wings. You're selfless, like the One who always uplifts, never expecting anything in return. Your presence among us reminds us to pay closer attention to those who are often unnoticed; your heart for the orphan, widow, and poor preaches a louder message than any sermon we might hear. Thank you for helping us catch a glimpse of the God who carries all of us close to his heart, who loves us in our brokenness, and will not let us go.

❧ SCRIPTURES FOR THE HUMBLE SOUL ❧

Read the following Scriptures, each accompanied by words to personalize this exercise. Notice the one with which you most resonate. Then softly read it aloud several times, write it out, and ponder it until you can almost recall it from memory. Over the coming days, find affirmation in knowing that you bring God's love into the world in meaningful ways, and that the Scriptures affirm your way of being in the world related to resources.

   ✐ I can help others in a financially responsible and compassionate way. The Bible says we should "live in harmony with one another. Do not be proud, but be willing to associate with people of low position. Do not be conceited" (Rom. 12:16).

- My compassion for others is confirmed by the Scriptures. "Finally, all of you, be like-minded, be sympathetic, love one another, be compassionate and humble" (1 Pet. 3:8).
- I can trust in the Lord, for I know "God opposes the proud but shows favor to the humble" (James 4:6).

REFLECTION QUESTIONS FOR AARON TYPES

- In what ways do you sacrifice financially for the benefit of others? How does this make you feel?
- Who else in your life is an Aaron type?
- With which of the core characteristics or stories about Aaron or Aaron types did you most resonate and why? How do you see yourself in light of this characteristic or story?
- Do you experience financial tension with certain people? If so, in what way might your Aaron money type contribute to this tension?
- What is one thing you plan to do differently with money now that you understand your Aaron money type?
- What is the greatest truth you've learned about the Aaron money type?

CHAPTER 8

DAVID—LEADERSHIP

*David said to Saul, "Let no one lose heart on
account of this Philistine; your servant will go and
fight him."*

1 SAM. 17:32

For forty days the Philistine behemoth, Goliath, stepped forward and cursed Israel's army and God's name. The enemy
warrior had established the terms of military engagement against
Israel. "Choose a man and have him come down to me. If he is able
to fight and kill me, we will become your subjects; but if I overcome him and kill him, you will become our subjects and serve us"
(1 Sam. 17:8–9).

There was no match for Goliath, in skill or stature; all Israelite
hands were tucked in pockets as no man stepped up to volunteer
for what appeared to be a suicide mission against the Philistine.
The options were not good: face the giant and die or send someone
else to face the giant; he'll lose and then you'll become a Philistine
slave—you and your family, that is. When terrorizing giants set

terms of battle, odds are you're in for a long haul up a steep hill, a hill you'll die on.

David—a young, ruddy, and handsome boy who was not old enough for battle—packed a lunch for his brothers, checked in his flock of sheep with a substitute shepherd, and headed for the front lines. He knew right where to find his kin; the giant had approached and taunted the army each day for over a month. He joined his brothers on the line, and sure as clockwork the Philistine champion made his snide remarks about David's fellow Israelites, his brothers, and his God. The men of Israel, who were gathered at the battle line and saw Goliath, fled in terror.

Back in the huddle they talked among themselves, perhaps trying to muster some level of confidence. "Do you see how this man keeps coming out? He comes out to defy Israel. The king will give great wealth to the man who kills him. He will also give him his daughter in marriage and will exempt his family from taxes in Israel" (v. 25). After having the Israelite soldiers repeat the terms of the reward, twice, David said to Saul, "Let no one lose heart on account of this Philistine; your servant will go and fight him" (v. 32).

Saul attempted to dissuade David, whom he assessed as incompetent to fight Goliath. There was, after all, a lot at stake if even one Israelite lost to the Philistine; it would affect the entire people of Israel, who would become slaves. However, David, even from a young age, had an impressive fight record, which he rattled off to the king. The problem was, all his fights were against animals like lions and bears that attempted to destroy his father's resources, his sheep. But David persuaded Saul, claiming the God who delivered him from the paws of predators would deliver him from Goliath. Saul sensed David's confidence and bid him well against the giant, clothing the boy with his own armor and weaponry.

Young David found the armor ill fitting, but more than that, it didn't support his fight style. David was a stone-slinger, not a sword-wielder. He dropped the armor, gripped his shepherd's staff, and grabbed five smooth stones from the wadi. The behemoth saw him coming and mocked him. David reached into his pouch, placed one stone in his sling, and raced to the battle line. He hurled the stone at the giant, and it sunk into his forehead, causing him to fall face-first onto the ground. Having no sword of his own, David severed the giant's head from his neck, using the Philistine's own sword to do the work.

Israel welcomed a new hero into its ranks that day, and children's bedtime storybooks gained a new chapter. David defeated Goliath with sling and stone, and his legacy was set in motion—the legacy of a boy who became a warrior, a leader, and eventually a king.

It was David's confidence in God, coupled with his comfort and competence with his weapons, that set him up for victory against Goliath. He leveraged the resources at his disposal, stones and a sling, to achieve victory and inspire followership. As we will see, he was also motivated to fight by the resources he would potentially gain for killing his foe. David led grown men, Israelite warriors, into battle against the Philistine ranks, not because of his position or title, but because he properly deployed resources, and faith, toward a singular goal—take down that giant. This is the work of leadership, and over his life's course, David continually inspired confidence and used resources to bring about incredible possibilities.

David represents God's leadership, which does not shrink back from formidable foes, but calls us to stand tall in the face of towering giants, whatever form they take. Like God, who countless times throughout Scripture helped the people of God overcome seemingly insurmountable foes or desperate situations, David led God's people toward their destiny. He reminded them why their lives mattered, inspired them with confidence, compelled them to act, and aligned resources to achieve desired goals. Resources, in the light of a leader with a vision, and in light of God, take on significance and meaning.

Basic Belief: Money Is a Tool to Create New Futures

The way of David is leadership. David types, with their formidable sense of destiny and intense passion, are able to inspire others to action, instilling them with confidence like David instilled in others upon defeating Goliath. David types are leaders at whatever they do, ranging from professional to more personal engagements, from the boardroom to the schoolyard to the athletic field. Any type can lead when it comes to money, but David types have a distinct ability to see the big picture. They possess a clear sense of why something is worth pursuing, and they align resources toward action.

In leadership roles, David types elicit followers because their goals are inspirational and inclusive; they cast a clear vision and welcome others to pursue it with them. Their financial visions and goals inspire followership and financial engagement because they appeal to a shared interest, not simply to a vision or goal that improves the leader's life alone. David types help others see why financial contribution toward a goal is worth investing their personal resources.

David types are inclined toward the future, toward what is

possible. Like David, whose life reveals that he possessed a strong sense of destiny, David types resist satisfaction with situations as they are, figuring out how to make incremental tweaks. Rather, David types explore and invent brand-new futures. They're blue-sky, big-time visionaries who spend far more time imagining what's next than focusing on what's happening right now. They set ambitious goals for their future, and they're rarely satisfied with life as it is. David types break new ground on a regular basis—they're always leaning toward the future, toward new possibilities. They tend to be singularly focused and highly driven.

Mark Rutland is a compelling example of a David type. He received the call to become president of a small Bible college, which was floundering financially and at risk of losing competitive edge and relevance. The college needed to change or it would die.

Mark possessed a clear vision for the college's future—one that was simultaneously unnerving and inspirational because it appeared nearly impossible. He sought to transform a dilapidated, tired campus with deteriorating facilities into a world-class, state-of-the-art training ground for the next generation of Christian leaders. The vision necessitated millions of dollars in capital improvements and a seismic shift in self-concept if the college were to regain relevance in a highly competitive and fast-changing higher education market.

Skeptics abounded, but Mark surrounded himself with a team of leaders and investors who caught his vision, which he shared at every opportunity through walking tours, site plans, and visionary talks. Within a few short years, energy and enthusiasm for the future returned; a sense of momentum began to build and donors invested in the next generation's education and training.

The aging facilities and classrooms were indeed transformed

into a sprawling, state-of-the-art campus that rivaled world-class resort destinations. Palm trees bordering cobblestone pathways replaced scrubby shrubs. The college achieved university status and changed its mascot, its brand, and its stature, becoming one of the fastest-growing private liberal arts colleges in the United States and garnering national attention. In many ways, Mark reinvented the category, or at least set the bar, for what it meant to be a Bible college.

A proven leader who is able to rally financial support for important projects, Mark thrives on challenge. The larger the stakes and the more imminent the threat, the more interested Mark appears. He's confident that, with God's help, anything is possible. He aligns resources toward a clear and compelling vision. Mark is a transformational leader and walks the way of David.

Core Characteristics of David Types

Driven by Why, They Inspire Action

We may be familiar with the story of young David running to the battle line armed with stones from the wadi. But we often overlook a part of the account: before David ran to do battle with Goliath, he *ran from* doing battle with Goliath. First Samuel 17:22–24 clearly depicts the scene. David ran to the battle lines to greet his brothers, Goliath came out, and everybody fled in terror—including David. It was not until David found his *why*—that is, his reason for fighting Goliath—that he returned to fight.

The narrative provides a few clues about why David stepped up. The giant mocked the name of the God of Israel, he mocked Israel's armies, and the financial reward for defeating the giant would change David's family's legacy forever (1 Sam. 17:25). These factors, combined with his faith in God, inspired David to act. When David discovered his *why*, there appeared to be no doubt in his mind about what he needed to do and that God would be with him.

A David type with a strong sense of *why* can become transformational, igniting others to action. When David discovered what was at stake financially for his family, he raced to the battle line and engaged his enemy. When he was victorious, all Israel followed suit. All the soldiers knew what was at stake, but none had found a strong enough *why* to inspire him to act. When David did, it changed everything, but not just for him. Something broke loose in the hearts of Israel's army, and they routed their enemy. David, driven by *why*, led the way by his actions, transforming a fearful army into ranks of victorious soldiers.

Those who have fallen on hard times are particularly drawn to David types because David types provide realistic opportunities for things to change—they instill hope. Far from hucksters who overpromise and underdeliver, David types make good on their promises. The plans they put in place, which sometimes require great faith and risk, are always achievable with God's help.

FINANCIAL LEADERS

David types inspire people to give money to important projects or opportunities. While we'll unpack this story further in a moment, it's important to recognize that Scripture shows us David was the primary fundraiser for Solomon's temple—a massive, expensive capital project that some speculate would cost in the billions of dollars in today's economy. His leadership abilities made him a prime candidate to lead people into financial engagement with such a monumental undertaking.

David types are able to cast a vision large enough that followers can find meaning for themselves within the vision, thereby making personal commitments to achieve it because they see potential in the future toward which the leader calls them. In this case, they understood the temple would serve God and God's people in worship. David types help others see why financial contribution toward a goal is worth personal sacrifice.

When fundraising, David types will often be the first to put up their own money toward a project. I learned this valuable lesson from Lauren.

"Why didn't you ask me to be the first person to make a gift to this project?" she inquired as I gathered my belongings and headed out the door of her office. We'd spent the last hour brainstorming funding strategies for renovating one of the church building's foyers, making it more accommodating to families with younger children. It would be costly to undertake. I knew Lauren had a heart for the next generation, even though her children were mature adults who'd left home long ago. I was seeking her insight into fundraising because she had experience in that area, not because I wanted her money.

I responded, "Because I'm not here to raise money today. I just wanted to discuss ideas for how we might pay for this project."

Lauren gave me a valuable lesson. "God has gifted some people with the desire and ability to both inspire others to give substantially to a project and do the same. If you have a compelling vision, people will resonate with it. You've spent the last hour imagining what's possible for the next generation, and I want to be part of that. Let me know when you figure out how I can help. By the way, one key to being successful at fundraising is being generous yourself. Never forget that." I heard much wisdom in that conversation that I will never forget.

As financial leaders, David types not only don't mind being asked to financially participate, they also long for the opportunity if the project is meaningful. In fact, they often want to be at the helm, laying the financial groundwork for a project others can build on, and which will inspire others to give financially to the project.

David types thrive off the thrill of being financial leaders, of being at the bleeding edge of a new idea or project. They experience deep satisfaction in knowing they were part of something significant and inspired others to act through their own participation.

Most successful fundraising projects will have principal or lead donors who contribute extensively to the project, even before the project goes public, so that it gains early momentum. That giving, then, draws other gifts to the table. David types usually rise to the surface in these cases, seeing potential and opportunity in a project that inspires their hearts and minds, even before many others know the project or opportunity exists. If they're not inspired to join the project, they'll clearly tell you. When they do resonate, however, they'll be one of your greatest assets toward the project's success.

SHARE THE SPOILS

David types are equitable financial leaders. When they gain success, they never take all the credit or financial gain for themselves. They're quick to return thanks to God and their comrades, and everybody shares in the spoils. David types are trustworthy to share financial gains with their teams, and they never use or abuse team members for their own financial well-being.

We see this characteristic emerge in David's life when the Amalekites swept Ziklag clean, taking everything in David's camp, including women and children. David's men wept until they wore themselves out; they were so emotionally distraught that they contemplated stoning David on the spot. But David sought strength in the Lord, inquired of Abiathar the priest about what he should do, and decided to pursue the band of Amalekite raiders. Fatigued and unable to keep up with David and many of the men, two hundred of David's company halted at the Wadi Besor; four hundred continued the search-and-recovery efforts, with David at the head. On getting a tip from an abandoned Amalekite slave as to the army's whereabouts, David and his men attacked the raiders, recovered the spoils, and rescued their wives and children.

Returning to Ziklag, David and the victorious men reunited with the two hundred men who did not cross the wadi. However, not everyone who went to battle with David was happy to see the two hundred who did not fight. Some among the victorious warriors spoke up, saying, "Because they did not go out with us, we will not share with them the plunder we recovered. However, each man may take his wife and children and go" (1 Sam. 30:22). David, however, proclaimed that the men who remained with the army's baggage would share in the spoils, and from that day on, the principle of equitable distribution among the warriors was fixed.

David types recognize the responsibility to maintain equitability, or a sense of financial fairness and reward, among followers. Rather than the C-suite garnering all the spoils of the company's success from a banner year, David types ensure that those who contributed to success share in the rewards. Because they recognize that victory comes from the Lord, David types are quick to distribute financial rewards among the people. For this reason, among many others, David's followers went to great lengths to ensure that he was always successful; they knew David's success contributed to their own success.

Businessman Don Flow has created a successful business based on this principle of equitability. The son of a car dealership owner, Flow inherited the family's business and stewarded a company that now employs over one thousand team members in over thirty franchises in North Carolina and Virginia. Every profession carries with it stereotypes, however justly or unjustly earned, and car dealerships and car salespeople are not known, on average, for being ethical and equitable in transactions. Flow's company believes this trend can change.

Flow works to create a strong culture of equitability in three spheres of influence: customers, team members, and community. With customers, Flow's company intentionally raises the level of transparency associated with each automobile deal so that, in Flow's words, they can hold true to the Proverbs, which assert that the vulnerable should not be taken advantage of. Further, they limit profit margins, regardless of what an under-informed customer would be willing to pay. Additionally, the company gives each employee three thousand dollars per year, per child, for that child's college tuition. On top of this, the company provides an emergency fund in the form of a grant that supports team members who fall on hard times. In the community, Flow's organization is at the helm of countless fundraising projects, and they also pay employees while they engage in volunteer efforts in the city—they view this as an investment in the company, whose goal is to invest in the community.

Flow believes financial leadership should result in followers' lives flourishing. Proper financial stewardship, evident when a David type is at the helm, maintains a sense of equitability that transforms environments from what they are to what they might become. Obviously, this requires more than the singular effort of a charismatic leader and his or her resources—it takes a collective effort of aligning energy and financial resources toward a vision that transcends self-interest and bottom lines.[18] For this reason, Flow is regularly invited to chair committees and projects in the community, using his David-type influence and resources to inspire others to action and to rally participation in noble causes.

OFTEN UNDERDOGS

David's life circumstances and story ignite courage in underdog hearts. He inspires those who have found themselves seeking financial change, those desiring to better their economic situation, to not recoil from a challenge just because failure seems likely.

Nobody would care if David randomly picked a fight with some big bully in the Philistine ranks and killed him. The circumstances that surrounded him, and the motivations that fueled his confidence, are the factors that make this particular fight interesting. Overlooked by his father when Samuel the prophet came to anoint the next king of Israel, disdained by his brothers when he arrived at the battlefield carrying provisions from home and expressed interest in the battle, David was never first on anyone's Most Likely to Succeed Sibling list. Readers may get the sense that David regularly found himself asking, "Now what did I do that's ticking everybody off?" (see 1 Sam. 17:29).

The biblical concept of *ultimogeniture* is a lofty word that expresses a simple, yet powerful scriptural theme that may help some readers understand why they identify so deeply with David. Essentially, *ultimogeniture* entails a younger sibling, one who should not rise to the top, receiving favor, inheritance, selection, or prevailing when an older sibling was the apparent choice or likely victor. In this case, David was a younger sibling who was appointed king of Israel, became victor and hero in battle, and rose to prominence. Such was also the case with Isaac, Jacob, Joseph, and many others. Even Israel, as a people, is viewed as the little apple of God's eye, the underdog people who faced impossible odds, and yet somehow succeeded when they trusted in the Lord. We love to see the underdog win, and Scripture loves to show that this happens when God is at work.

David is the consummate underdog because of his stature and status—he's too small to fit into Saul's armor and his father fails to present him to Samuel as a valid option for Israel's next king. David, by all measures, didn't measure up—too small, too young, too annoying to siblings, too whatever. Apparently, David didn't get the message that he was underqualified for battle. He'd victoriously faced wild animals while protecting his father's sheep. God spared and empowered David then, and David believed God would surely do so now. David's story teaches us that when underdogs face seemingly insurmountable obstacles, if there's a clear vision for the future, a strong why, and trust in God, nothing is impossible.

DESIRE TO LEAVE A FINANCIAL LEGACY
FOR THE NEXT GENERATION

The next generation remains a top priority for David types, so while they charge ahead toward their goals, they're always reaching back to the younger generation and bringing them along. David types may have come from humble beginnings, perhaps often overlooked and ill equipped by most people's standards. But either somebody gave them an opportunity to succeed or they overcame the odds and rose to the top. So David types pay it forward, making sure the next generation doesn't start from financial scratch.

True leadership leaves a legacy the next generation can build upon. David types set the next generation up for financial success.

My friend John, who is in his mid-sixties and tends toward the David type, took me out for coffee one day. "You do realize I'm going to die, don't you?" he began. John looked fit as ever. I feared he'd been given some bad news by his doctor.

"John, what's going on?"

"Nothing," he replied. "I'm going to die; you're going to die; that baby over there in the corner in the high chair is going to die. That's how it goes. But I have this question—how big are your dreams? And how do we raise up the next generation to achieve them? If we pursue only our best ideas, and not God's dreams for this city, the next generation won't resonate with them. We'll be like a football team who gets all the way to the end zone and turns around and punts the ball the wrong way, forcing the next generation to reclaim the ball and advance it yet again. We'll make progress but then lose it unless we raise up the next generation to pursue God's dreams for this city."

John puts his money where his mouth is. He's deeply financially engaged with projects in our city that position the next generation of civic and religious leaders to succeed. While John has completed a successful professional career, which entailed pastoring a church, leading a Christian school, sitting on every imaginable civic board and council, and eventually becoming mayor, his vision for the future is clearer than ever. His only hope is that he lives long enough to see his heart's dreams materialize. Until they become reality, he's spending his days investing in young leaders who can carry the ball across the line.

We see this same heart for setting the next generation up to win in David's life. David said to Solomon, "My son, I had it in my heart to build a house for the Name of the LORD my God. But this word of the LORD came to me: '. . . You are not to build a house for my Name . . . But you will have a son . . . He is the one who will build a house for my Name'" (1 Chron. 22:7–10).

One final dream resided within David's heart. He'd slayed lion and bear, giant and enemy armies, avoided assassination attempts from friend and foe, and now, nearing his life's end, he desired rest. More than that, he wanted a resting place for the ark that symbolized God's covenant with the people. David took the people as far as he could go, but because his greatest dream was wrapped up in God's ever-unfolding story in the earth, he would never lay his head to rest knowing all had been accomplished. David's dreams were never really his; they were God's dreams, and David played a part in their being realized. God's dreams, however, are always bigger than our life spans, vaster than what any human can ask or imagine. David realized his life was ending, but God's dreams were ever unfolding.

David knew Solomon wasn't prepared to build the temple. Understanding the challenge clearly, he thought to himself, "My son Solomon is young and inexperienced, and the house to be built for the LORD should be of great magnificence and fame and splendor in the sight of all the nations. Therefore I will make preparations for it" (v. 5).

The list of building materials David amassed was staggering and included one million talents of silver and "more bronze than could be weighed" (v. 3). In short, David went all out and spared no personal expense in bringing materials to the job site. He leveraged every relationship he had and called for every willing heart to make a freewill offering to the Lord so everything needed to commence with groundbreaking was ready, in advance.

David did more than provide the materials for his son to build the temple. He laid the political framework Solomon could stand on. David charged his officials to follow Solomon's leadership at every turn. He explained that Solomon was inexperienced—everyone knew this, and David spoke to the challenge in everyone's mind, positioning Solomon as the heir apparent to the Davidic throne, the anointed and chosen one selected by God's own hand. David knew Solomon would face insurmountable challenges following in the footsteps of such a famous and accomplished military and political leader as himself. The only way God would get glory through the building of the temple would be for David to set up the next generation of leadership for victory, provide everything they needed for success, and then step out of the way.

To this day, people refer to the temple as Solomon's temple, not David's temple. In reality, David advanced the plan to one foot shy of the finish line; Solomon took it the rest of the way. Solomon gets credit for the temple; David did all the heavy lifting. The point, however, is well put by David—getting credit for the temple belonged to God. God needed no house, but the temple would serve as a way for the people to more intimately relate to God, and as a means for onlookers to see the awe and wonder the people of Israel had for their God. As alluring as structures can be to sweep worship and attention toward the edifice and away from God's face, the motivation for building the temple, as recorded in Scripture, seems directed at God receiving glory.

When it was time to move the project ahead, David called out to the people, "'Who then will offer willingly, consecrating himself today to the LORD?' . . . Then the people rejoiced because they had given willingly, for with a whole heart they had offered freely to the LORD. David the king also rejoiced greatly" (29:5, 9

ESV). Nothing brings joy to a David type's heart like seeing the next generation succeed and for God to get the glory. God's legacy, not a David type's legacy, is what enables a David type's heart to rejoice *greatly*.

Solomon finished building the temple. The chroniclers state that Solomon became great in the eyes of all Israel, and no king before him had the regal majesty Solomon possessed (v. 25). The next paragraph records that David died at a ripe old age, and his son Solomon reigned in his stead. David succeeded as a leader because his successor was set up for victory, and the way he used his money made this possible.

David types, long before they pass off the scene, leave a financial legacy that transcends the amount afforded to heirs in trust funds or inheritances. First and foremost, the legacy is one of a woman or man who honors the Lord and seeks God's fame and glory above her or his own. Then, because God is first in a David type's heart, this person's resources are devoted to the Lord's work in the earth, setting up the next generation with the resources necessary to carry out the vision. Because David types always remember that God raised them up, and one day they will go the way of all the earth and leave everything to someone else, they embrace the next generation's inabilities and inexperience, hand off the plans, and bid them to listen to what God wants to do in and through them now.

Shadow Side: Selfishness

Selfishness, the shadow side of David-type leadership, is the antithesis of what endeared so many to the selfless king who was known for marching at the head of his army to battle. When leadership turns bad, it uses the charisma and influence it possesses to acquire resources for selfish, self-serving purposes, whether those are human or material resources. At its best, David-type leadership would never pair the terms *human* and *resources*, because humans are more than resources; humans are the image of God. David types, when operating from their shadow sides, devalue the people for whom they would otherwise give their lives.

In the extreme, David types can become so focused on what they want—on what they don't have now and desire in their future—that they run past or over cherished relationships, friends, family, and so on. Because David types are strongly future-oriented, they can lose sight of the goodness of life as it is.

Selfishly Use People and Resources

Readers might recall a number of David's exploits, notable among them the time he stayed home when kings traditionally go out to battle and slept with another man's wife. From the comfort of his room he spotted Bathsheba, a lovely young woman who was taking a bath. Her beauty incited the king to tell his attendants to bring her to him. As a result of their union, she conceived a child. David had Bathsheba's husband, Uriah (one of his army), brought home from battle so the pregnancy would appear to be his doing, not David's. When her husband showed more character than the king and slept outside in solidarity with his comrades who were still on the battlefield, David had the commander of his army send Uriah to the front lines of battle, where he was killed.

David types, when they give in to their shadow sides, become selfish and self-centered, even doing harm to others to get what they want. As mentioned earlier, many David types have rags-to-riches stories, and whether or not they've achieved any substantial level of financial wealth, they are the type constantly striving toward a future that is so clear in their minds they can practically touch it. They're relentless toward success because they remember where they came from and want to change their financial future. Perhaps they fear losing control, being passed over for a promotion, or sliding into insignificance. Maybe they have a deep fear of experiencing a severe blow to their financial stability.

Whatever the impetus, David types will move heaven and earth to make certain they do not fail, that they get what they want. Because their success is so much a part of their identity, David types interpret failure, particularly financial failure, as personal failure, as though *they* are a failure.

One David type I met turned toward the shadows when she allowed her position of financial influence to cloud her judgment. She grew her financial asset base from nothing to millions, lost it all (a couple of times because she aggressively borrowed money to finance risky investments), and rebuilt her portfolio to an unfathomable level of wealth. As we waited while technicians changed the oil in her car, the conversation drifted to her church's engagement with an organization that built schools in third-world countries. She lamented, "The church is always asking me for money. If they weren't always trying to solve every problem in the world, they'd be able to focus on this community and actually do something worthwhile here." Perhaps she had a point. The church, while large and influential, tended to cherry-pick *feel good* causes from around the globe, sending short-term vacationaries to deliver goods and take a lot of photos to display on Sundays.

Because she was a savvy businesswoman, the church's marketing tactics didn't impress her. However, what she said next floored me.

"The reason this country where we're building a school is in the ditch is because their leaders take advantage of them. Other countries take advantage of them. If our country wants to stay on top, *we will have to take advantage of them*. We need to be drilling for oil, not building a school. They'll just take the money we're sending it and waste it!" (Cue the crickets, awkwardness, and my scrambling for how to respond.) She'd allowed her influence and wealth to cloud her judgment; power corrupted her sense of moral agency, responsibility, and boundaries. She'd become self-centered and selfish.

Can Become Complacent

While David types are future-oriented, when they succeed they run the risk of growing too comfortable. They can spend too much time taking stock of their own successes; they can become complacent. First Chronicles 21:1 records that Satan incited David to take a census and number the children of Israel. This matter displeased the Lord, and great harm fell on the people of Israel. While David repented of the act, many lost their lives when their leader numbered the people of Israel. In this context, the narrator does not account for why David numbered the people, nor does he say why this displeased the Lord. But we can infer that numbering one's subjects turns people into data, and shifts one's trust in the Lord to trusting in the number of people at one's disposal to provide continued success and security.

David types are at their best when they are following the Lord and doing kingdom work, not when they are sending others to do their bidding for them, and certainly not when they are counting heads (or dollars) when they should be leading at the head of the people. The most dangerous moment in a leader's life presents itself when he or she has recently experienced a significant victory. When David types become comfortable with their accomplishments, they should seek what the Lord wants them to be engaged with next, how they can set the next generation up for victory, rather than simply relishing in the comfort that their prior successes have brought about.

Growing in Financial Well-Being

Embrace Your Desire to Create New Futures with Money

You're always advancing, seeking the next frontier or new venture, and you believe money is a tool to help you achieve inspiring possibilities. You're a forerunner, and that intimidates some people. It's easy for others to critique your motives, to label you as overly ambitious and self-seeking. They don't understand your heart. Remember, David's brothers criticized him, and his father completely overlooked his potential. David, however, clung to the sense that, with God, all things are possible. True leaders, like David types, don't view themselves as all that important. The vision is what matters; the future beckons them onward, and they use money to create and fund those possibilities.

David actually lived a lonely existence, even though he was surrounded by those he led. It's rare that onlookers will totally understand you, because you're always out in front of the present; they may catch your vision, but by the time they do you're already contemplating what's next. This is the personal cost of leadership— you are always out front, and this can be a lonely existence at times, even if only internally.

It's said that God loves us as we are but refuses to leave us that way. If there's truth in this, it's because God sees what is possible—God is God of the living, of the present, but is continually leading followers into a redemptive future. This is how we see God in you; you remind us of the Lord, who inspires us with what is possible.

Use your money toward the dreams God has put in your heart; refuse to settle for what is when you know what can be. Your financial leadership is about more than your own life, and whether or not we catch your vision at the onset, we need you to keep pressing on. Embrace your desire to create new futures with money.

Focus on Legacy

Remember, it is God who has gifted you in financial leadership and raised you up. Will you partner with the Lord's work in someone else's life and raise them up? How will you set the next generation up for financial stability and victory? Do so by leaving more than a financial inheritance; leave a legacy. Intentionally seek those you can pour your energy into, thereby providing a platform on which they can stand taller and see farther.

Keep Your *Why* Clear and in Focus

Clarify your financial goals, and most important, why they matter to you. Then when you succeed at achieving them, you will avoid the pitfall of making success about yourself, and you'll cast a vision broad enough that others can join you. You're a strong leader, and you're likely to achieve your goals. If you don't keep in clear focus why you're after what you seek, you're more likely to make the pursuit and the goal about yourself. Besides, your *why* is what fuels your passion to succeed. Remain crystal clear on why you're doing what you're doing. If it helps, list a clear *why* related to each goal. Revisit it often, and you'll find inspiration to persevere and limit the chance that you'll drift from your mission.

DRAW YOUR BOUNDARIES; GUARD THEM CAREFULLY

Your leadership and influence with money will open all manner of doors of opportunity to you. Be careful which ones you enter. You need to establish clear boundaries that you will not transgress when it comes to money, and which will also safeguard you against others who seek to take advantage of you. Some companies have decided to close one day per week to allow employees a day of rest and worship; others stand firm on corporate policies that grate against the prevailing culture.

What are your financial boundaries? David established equitable rules for his troops when he returned from battle, sharing the spoils with the entire army and not just those who were actively engaged in battle. Don Flow made a policy about employee benefits that provided tuition for college. Are there certain things you will, and will not, do with money? Will you always donate a certain percentage to charity? Will you always seek to do good for one college student each year? If you don't know what your boundaries are financially, it's unlikely they'll guard your character when needed most. It's more likely that when you succeed you won't share the financial success with others because you've not set your personal financial policies in advance.

DETERMINE NOW TO GUARD AGAINST SELFISHNESS BY BEING GENEROUS

At their best, David types focus on leaving a legacy and raising up the next generation. At their worst, selfishness in David types tempts them to hoard rewards or become complacent. David types can lose sight of this and make financial endeavors all about themselves. When given influence over others from a financial standpoint, clearly articulate boundaries and opportunities for shared success so others can hold you accountable. Make the vision plain so others can rally with you toward a preferred future. This way, it will be more difficult to rest in your success while others go to battle on your behalf, and it will prevent you from exploiting others financially.

Remember, You Are Not What You Earn

Remain cautious of too closely identifying financial success with personal success, whether that's starting a new company that brings big profits or reaching your retirement goal early. You are not what you earn. You are not your successes. Your goals should emerge from your heart and sense of destiny; however, they must remain at a careful distance from the core of your being. You must almost view your goals as separate from your deepest sense of self.

While it's hard to imagine for some, it is not unusual that David types will set a lofty financial goal, reach it early, and then set an even higher goal. If their goal was to have a net worth of nine million dollars by age thirty-eight, and they reach that goal by age thirty-four, they'll just raise the goal even higher and keep striving. In some sense, what David types enjoy is the pursuit of the goal, not actually the number goal itself.

As a David type, when will you ever have enough? Do you have a net-worth number in mind that, when reached, will finally be enough, or a retirement date set in clear view? Consider the last time you were actually satisfied. Is it difficult to do? If so, it could be because you spend so much time living in the future that you forgo the opportunity to be satisfied in the present. As an Isaac type, I'm regularly asking, "What's wrong?" or "How can this be improved?" I'm motivated by a sense that things can be better or maximized. As a David type, you're likely asking, "What's missing?" or "What's next?" You're motivated by a sense that something is lacking, that something more is possible. Take a look around—you have much to be thankful for in this very moment. The opportunities to be grateful are endless.

FROM DRIVEN TO DELIGHT: A DAVID TYPE EMBRACES HIS DESIGN

Carl has a brilliant mind for making lots of money. "I'll never forget the first year I earned one hundred thousand dollars," he told me. "I thought I was king of the world. In those days, that amount of money was worth more than it is now. Then I set a five-year goal of earning five hundred thousand dollars annually, and when I eclipsed that mark, one million became my goal. I did the work; I achieved the goals." As he finished this statement, a nurse walked into the room, interrupting our dialogue.

"Mr. Jenkins, it's lunchtime. I'm going to lean your bed up so you can eat." Carl forced a smile without saying a word. He didn't enjoy receiving help from anyone. He played it all off in his typical, charismatic way.

"When I get out, I'm bringing my wife back here on Friday nights. The grilled chicken and mashed potatoes are to die for." He turned his head toward the nurse. "Do you all take reservations?"

Carl would get out soon enough, and he'd carry with him a new diet, exercise plan, and a small scar where the surgeon performed heart surgery. More than that, he'd take away a renewed focus on life and finances. His heart attack nearly triggered a payout on his life insurance policy to his wife. He knew he'd narrowly escaped.

"Building my own empire doesn't matter to me like it did before. I want to do something that counts," he candidly confessed. We spent the morning together, talking about what matters and why it makes a difference. Carl knew he needed to dial things back; his pace was out of control. He was always charging ahead, which he enjoyed at some level, but he was wearing himself out in the process. His health hiccup got his attention.

As we discussed the characteristics of his David money type, it was extremely important that rather than shunning his desire to use money to bring about new possibilities, we needed to clarify and focus it. He'd grown so accustomed to succeeding with all his financial ventures that he confused financial success for financial meaning. Now his focus shifted from *what makes the most money* to *what makes money that makes the most difference*. He still had plenty of years left on his life's odometer, so he wanted to make the next couple of decades count.

We spent time revisiting his *why*, which led to a renewed focus, sense of energy, and commitment to direct his attention only to opportunities that aligned with his *why*. Carl didn't need more money; he needed to reconnect with why making money mattered, and he created three boundaries that kept the wrong opportunities out and let the right ones in:

- ✿ Does this opportunity seem like fun to me?
- ✿ Will this opportunity require me to compromise my values or health in any way?
- ✿ Does this opportunity make a difference in the lives of my team, community, and the next generation?

Today, Carl's boundaries guard his financial well-being, and he's still making money in the process.

🌿 A Blessing for David Types 🌿

We see God in you as we watch you inspire and lead us— you call out to what is possible. You have such a heart for the next generation, reminding us of the God of Abraham, Isaac, and Jacob—the God who sees the next generation in line. You care deeply about what lies ahead, yet you won't forget those who'll follow in your footsteps—you make us feel important, like we're part of something larger than ourselves. One generation commends the kingdom to another, and you compel us to not forsake the Lord, who is our source and strength of all that is possible. You see potential in us, calling out to the best and brightest in each life, and compelling us to go God's way together.

🌿 Scriptures for the Leading Soul 🌿

Read the following Scriptures, each accompanied by words that personalize this exercise. Notice the one with which you most resonate. Then softly read it aloud several times, write it out, and ponder it until you can almost recall it from memory. Over the coming days, find affirmation in knowing that you bring God's love into the world in meaningful ways, and that the Scriptures affirm your way of being in the world related to resources.

- My goal is to lead with financial integrity, knowing that "a good name is more desirable than great riches; to be esteemed is better than silver or gold" (Prov. 22:1).
- Everything I need comes from God's good hand.

Regardless of my financial successes or failures, I trust knowing that "the LORD is my shepherd; I lack nothing" (Ps. 23:1).

- When it comes to money, leadership means I will "do to others as [I] would have them do to [me]" (Luke 6:31).

REFLECTION QUESTIONS FOR DAVID TYPES

- In what ways do you find yourself leading others financially? How does this make you feel?
- Who else in your life is a David type?
- With which of the core characteristics or stories about David or David types did you most resonate and why? How do you see yourself in light of this characteristic or story?
- Do you experience financial tension with certain people? If so, in what way might your David money type contribute to this tension?
- What is one thing you plan to do differently with money now that you understand your David money type?
- What is the greatest truth you've learned about the David money type?

CHAPTER 9

THE WAY TO FINANCIAL WELL-BEING

When you discover in yourself something that is a gift from God, you have to claim it and not let it be taken away from you. Sometimes people who do not know your heart will altogether miss the importance of something that is part of your deepest self, precious in your eyes as well as God's . . . It is then that you have to speak your heart and follow your deepest calling.[19]
HENRI NOUWEN

The way to financial well-being is a returning home to your deepest sense of self, which is rooted and nurtured in God's love. So much financial teaching begins from the outside and sometimes works its way in. If you've made it to this point in the book, you've done the hard, heart-level work of tending to your interior life so when you consider the ways you handle money, you know why you act the way you do. You've discovered more about who you are and how God has designed you. Now you can see beyond the traditional notions that people must fit a specific money mold and that there is only one right way to think and feel about finances. The way you relate to money stems from the way you relate to God, from the unique way you are God-wired to encounter the world and its resources.

Understanding that it is God who has designed you to think, feel, and act the way you do financially gives you the courage to embrace your type, while continually growing and maturing in how you relate to God and money. Once you've embraced your own type, you'll create space for others to be who they are, and you'll be positioned to understand them and relate to them in a way that enhances your own, and their own, financial well-being.

Embracing Your Type

You're free to embrace your money type when you understand that no one type is better than another, and that God designed each type. This realization gives you permission to listen to your own financial thoughts, emotions, and actions and discern how God has designed you and may want you to grow in your relationship to money.

For example, hospitality, the Abraham type, is not better than discipline, the Isaac type. Nor is connection, the Joseph type, better than leadership, the David type. All seven types, with their strengths and the lessons they teach us, round out the human experience; each inspires us to grow and mature, and together they create a more complete picture of God's image.

OVERVIEW OF THE SEVEN MONEY TYPES

Type	Aspect of God's Image	Basic Belief	Key Characteristic	Shadow Side	Well-Being Growth
Abraham	Hospitality	Money should be used to make others feel special and valued	Loves using money on gifts and serving others	Self-sufficiency: has difficulty receiving from others	Remember to spend on yourself
Isaac	Discipline	Money should not be wasted but rather maximized	Makes the most of every dollar	Fear: is afraid resources will run out	Lighten up; plan to splurge
Jacob	Beauty	Money should be used to create pleasurable experiences	Enjoys using money to create beautiful moments or buy beautiful things	Indulgence: over-spends on desirable items or experiences	Become more intentionally others-centered in your spending
Joseph	Connection	Money makes connections possible and opens doors	Uses money to forge important relational connections and partnerships	Manipulation: uses money and relationships for self-centered gain	Learn to limit the number of financial commitments
Moses	Endurance	Money should be carefully ordered	Loves financial order, budgets, and a good plan	Impatience: is aggravated at wastefulness and lack of planning	Create space between self and finances; disengage and rest
Aaron	Humility	Money should be used to serve others	Concerned for injustices/needs and spends to remedy them	Instability: has a lack of planning and attention to finances	Resist cynicism toward financial planning
David	Leadership	Money is a tool to create new futures	Invests in the next generation; financial leaders	Selfishness: forgets financial success was a team effort	Set clear financial boundaries to maintain integrity

It's been my experience that most religious financial teachings stem from a deep appreciation for the Abraham, Isaac, Moses, and Aaron types. You'll hear much Abraham-type teaching about the role of giving hospitably to others and religious institutions so you can get a financial or spiritual blessing in return. Isaac and Moses types talk about getting your financial household in order to make the most of every dollar and Aaron types can make you feel guilty for not giving all your money away and living with no future financial plans.

Each emphasis has some measure of truth. However, those who espouse these views as "the right way God wants you to handle money" don't account for the diversity of God's design. They don't see that there are seven unique and wonderful ways of worshipping God with the way a person uses money. We need to celebrate all seven types because God created them all, and only when all work together do we get a fuller image of what it means to be truly human.

We would never read the story of Moses and expect it to mimic David's story, for example. We read each of these stories because they're unique, even if from time to time they overlap in the lessons they teach. This is true of our lives, and true of the money types. While similarities exist between all of them, there's something special about each one. Rather than feeling inferior or superior because of how we relate to money, which results in internal tension, we must embrace the types and find compassion for one another, seeing God at work in diverse ways, helping one another grow and mature. This leads to financial well-being; this resolves financial tensions. We must build up one another in our strengths, bearing with one another in our weaknesses. In this way we can learn from one another, hold one another accountable, and accomplish greater things together.

Resolving Internal Financial Tensions

Because each type brings with it both strengths and growth areas, both light and shadow, and because you now have a better understanding of the seven types, you'll become increasingly aware when you're experiencing competing thoughts and emotions that arise from the different aspects of God's image at play within you. Because we are all meant to grow in each of the seven types, and because each type is resident within all of us to some degree, some times will feel more challenging than others when it comes to money.

I'm often aware when my internal drive to maximize resources, typical of an Isaac type, conflicts with my God-given desire to sacrifice financially for the sake of others. The latter is a virtue all of us can and should embrace in a healthy way, but which comes most intuitively to Abraham and Aaron types. I can feel a longing within my being that wants me to forgo my own desires and sacrifice financially for the sake of another person, project, or cause, and yet my Isaac sensibilities regularly call me to analyze the situation, making certain the recipient is worthy. The Isaac tendencies often win out. When I slow down, considering how my most natural tendencies may be crowding out other good and godly instincts, I'm able to make decisions that reflect the fullness of who I am and hope to become, not just my primary money type.

I'm also able to be more patient with myself. Earlier in my life I would heap guilt on my own head, thinking I was just a greedy, self-centered person. I have learned to embrace my Isaac tendencies, which certainly can and do give generously, while opening my heart to grow in other areas. We can, and should, grow in each of the seven money types.

Marian is an example of someone who has learned to integrate money types so they work together. She strongly identifies with the Jacob and Moses types. Jacob represents beauty, and Jacob types can tend to go all out on purchasing items that bring pleasure, a wonderful experience, or beauty in general into the world. A Jacob type's first inclination is not to ask, "What does this cost?" but "How can I get what I want?"

Now, as mentioned, Marian's other inclination is toward the Moses type, which represents endurance, and Moses types operate off a well-organized budget, making sure every dollar knows its place.

Once Marian understood that she most resonates with these two types, it helped her understand her relationship with money. In her own words, "When I see something I want, whether it's a piece of art, new music, a pair of jeans, or the opportunity to attend a new production at the symphony, my heart begins to race—I get really excited. I'll figure out a way to get what I want, but the whole time I'm running the numbers in my head; I know exactly how much money I have in my checking account, when I get paid, and how to make it all work. Before I understood my strongest money types, I felt internally divided. Now I'm able to listen to my life and act in a responsible way, one that brings joy to my soul while not harming my financial position."

Marian has learned how her Jacob- and Moses-type tendencies can balance each other. Because she's aware of her type structure, she recognizes the thoughts and emotions that arise from each type. She's aware that the strengths of the Moses type, a desire for financial order, help her guard against the shadow side of a Jacob type, which can blow a budget in a hurry.

At the same time, she's listening to her Jacob-type sensibilities, which value beauty, aesthetics, and experiences, while not letting the more miserly tendencies of a Moses type, from its shadow side, suck the joy out of life. Awareness of how strongly you resonate with each type, along with understanding both the strengths and shadow side of that type, can bring clarity to why you think, feel, and act the way you do financially.

Understanding Others Better

As we have seen, the way to financial well-being involves embracing how we are uniquely designed, while opening our lives up to grow and mature related to finances. We will not be able to embrace others as they are, with their unique money types, until we've embraced the reality that we are deeply loved and astonishingly created by God, even amid our imperfections. As Jesus teaches, love your neighbor *as yourself*—you'll never embrace the uniqueness in another person until you've embraced who you are and how God wired you at your core (Mark 12:31).

When we see only darkness within ourselves, we'll project that darkness onto others. We'll never be able to properly relate to the resources we hold in our hands and to others with whom we interact financially until we've embraced the best of who we are, until we see God in ourselves and God at work in our finances. When we've awakened to God's love, which designed us cell and soul, our hearts are free to see both the goodness and beauty in the mirror image in front of us and our neighbor beside us. The more we see God in the ways we handle money, the clearer we see God at work in the deepest parts of our beings.

When you begin to understand your own money type, you'll also become more aware of how money types influence other people's behavior. As you give yourself permission to embrace your money type and to grow as you learn more about your unique design, you'll gain a greater capacity for compassion. You'll be better able to enter into another person's perspective in a way that affirms their unique way of relating to money. When you do, it will give you an increased ability to understand rather than judge other types.

Understanding your own type and having compassion for other types plays a crucial role in resolving financial tensions you may experience with others. That is a key component of your own financial well-being. If you're fighting about money, there's a good chance someone has failed to view the situation through another type's lens.

For example, early in our marriage, my wife and I argued most Saturday mornings for years. This was, for better or worse, the most convenient time we had to go over our budget, track receipts, and pay bills. More than one weekend was blown to pieces by the verbal grenades we lobbed back and forth at each other across our budget. After a while, we realized we tended to argue over one line item in particular: gifts given.

Gifts given was shorthand for the amount of money we budgeted each month to spend on gifts. Some months the number needed to be larger than others, at least in Elizabeth's mind, because we had more birthdays or anniversaries in our extended families to celebrate. I was firmly convinced that twenty-five dollars per month was more than enough to spend on gifts if Elizabeth would only plan well, shop for deals, be creative in her purchases, and even enlist the children in making, for example, birthday presents for grandparents, aunts, uncles, cousins, and so on. After all, who can't appreciate a hand-drawn piece of art from a toddler or a five-dollar gift card along with a ten-dollar-off coupon to a favorite store? I mean, let's get creative here, right? That's a fifteen-dollar gift for an anniversary present that only cost us five dollars. With twenty-five dollars per month, we could give five gifts of that sort with a little creativity and planning!

You can see why I drove her nuts.

You'll recall that I most identify with the Isaac type, who will squeeze every ounce of opportunity from resources. If you give Isaac types twenty-five dollars per month to spend on gifts, they'll figure out a way to give gifts to everyone they think is deserving and still have money left over, feel really good about that, and then put that extra cash in savings. My wife most identifies with the Abraham type. She freely and generously gives to others. She takes little thought for herself and is always seeking to understand how another person can be shown love or appreciation through the way she uses money. A classic Abraham type, she'll dip into her own allowance in the budget and spend that money on others, buying clothes as gifts when she actually needs a new pair of jeans.

None of this desire to maximize on my part or to give to others while personally having unmet desires on her part had anything to do with our expendable income—we weren't behind on bills or overly strapped for cash, thank God. It had everything to do with two unique, diverse money types learning to play nice in the same budget.

When an Isaac type and an Abraham type meet to discuss spending money on gifts, that line in the budget can become a line in the sand, and for those who are aware, that line has an arrow on the end that actually points beyond the numbers to something that resides deep in the core of each person's soul. For years I thought my wife was being frivolous, always having to give extravagant (by my standards) gifts and having to do so for every birthday and anniversary in the known universe. At the same time, she thought I was a cold-hearted, unfeeling, insensitive jerk when it came to giving gifts. Why was I being so cheap? Why was she being so irresponsible? It wasn't until we awakened to the unique ways God designs people to relate to money that we were able to find some compromise in this area of our finances.

Jean Vanier writes,

> The mature heart listens for what another's heart is meant to be. It no longer judges or condemns. It is a heart of forgiveness. Such a heart is a compassionate heart that sees the presence of God in others. It lets itself be led by them into uncharted land. It is the heart that calls us to grow, to change, to evolve, and to become more fully human.[20]

At first, I could not see the activity of God at work in Elizabeth's life by the way she related to money, especially as it pertained to giving generous gifts to others. I was unknowingly blinded by my own money type and conditioning, by my shadow side and financial training. The more I tried to impress upon her that she should adopt my line of thinking, the more we fought, and enjoyed Saturdays less, and the more she shriveled up on the inside related to money.

It was not until I began to take steps her way, to realize that my way of relating to money was not the only way of relating to money, that we began to fight less and enjoy Saturdays more. We began to talk honestly about how we felt and thought about money—my fears and hers, my dreams and hers—and experienced a newfound compassion for each other.

My Isaac-type tendencies lean toward the shadows of fear,

thus I regularly wanted to save or invest every extra dollar for a rainy day, thinking there may not be enough when I needed it. Elizabeth's Abraham type focused on the special occasion right in front of her; her heart went out to each person whom we had an opportunity to celebrate. She could not see how having a budget we were continually blowing, even though we could cover the overages in other areas, led to anxiety for me while these expenses produced joy for her.

We did more than give in to each other's desires—we found compassion for each other. I couldn't see that I was robbing Elizabeth of one of her greatest joys in life, and she couldn't see that all I wanted to do was make certain our family was financially stable, both then and in the future. I needed to get off the gas a bit with our monthly savings and create more opportunity for Elizabeth to express her desire to create meaningful experiences for others through giving gifts, and Elizabeth needed to understand there would never be a *gifts given* budget large enough to do what she wanted to do, so she'd need to work within less generous, agreed-upon boundaries. By understanding each other's money types, and by knowing each type's shadow side, we were able to grow in understanding and eventually to express compassion toward each other, celebrating and affirming rather than infuriating each other. This understanding increased each of our senses of financial well-being; we both felt affirmed, and our marriage was strengthened in the process.

Now you'll hear one of us say to the other, "All right, Abraham, we're going a little over the top here" or "Isaac, we've saved for this vacation for months. It's time to stop maximizing every dollar and enjoy yourself." This sends the message that we understand where the other is coming from, even if we're asking the other to change course. Most exciting to us now is that we're beginning to discern the unique ways our children relate to money, and now that we know where they're coming from, we'll be better prepared to steward their financial maturity. In little Seth we have the makings of an Isaac type, while Seri seems to walk the way of Jacob.

GOD WORKS IN AND AROUND YOU THROUGH MONEY TYPES

Money can be a divisive matter. Amounts often determine power, and power determines who is right and wrong. This is why we need to understand money types—both our own and other people's types.

Embracing your money type allows you to remain more confident and at peace in any financial situation; it allows you to embrace your relationship to money as a good part of your life, and especially your life in light of God. The moment you embrace your own type, by default you become increasingly aware that your type is one of seven, and that God is at work in diverse and unique ways in the lives of those around you. These realizations increase your chances of resolving both internal and relational financial tensions, and position you for a greater experience of financial well-being.

CONCLUSION

Some topics are deemed personal and not fit for open discourse in certain settings, and money exists on that list, perhaps alongside religion and sexuality. It's been this way since the beginning of time; religion, resources, and sexuality are the areas where we struggle most to find meaning and wholeness. So in our culture, we don't often talk about money, except perhaps when we go to the bank or make a purchase. Or when we've come into a lot of it or when we don't have enough of it, and then, often, we fight about it.

This is why understanding your money type is vital—it's a core component of becoming whole, of experiencing financial well-being in your life.

I love returning to the garden of Eden narrative because it depicts humanity's most essential dreams and fears in a simple, poetic manner. After all, the book of Genesis refers to the beginning, the story of creation we read to children, and it's the story that helps us make sense of who we are, why we exist, and what is possible with God. The dew-drenched ground of new creation in Genesis 1 begins to groan as the page turns to tragedy in Genesis 3. Here, our dreams are dashed, and we discover why we wrestle with life as we do; we glimpse that struggling with resources lies at the core of our oldest faith story.

Adam and Eve wrestled with their trust in God's promises when the serpent tempted them with the idea that God was withholding knowledge from them in the forbidden fruit, and that by eating it they'd become like God. For the first time humankind contemplated the thought that what we had, both with God and with our resources, was not enough.

After eating the fruit, Adam and Eve found themselves naked and ashamed of their bodies, encountering for the first time a sense of otherness and shamefulness in their sexuality, alienated from each other, blaming each other. The story tells us humankind would thereafter work the earth and it would resist producing. We wrestle to this day with these issues—getting the results we desire from our work, and receiving from our efforts what we think our labor is worth is a problem as old as time. These tensions are at the core of our relational, professional, and religious challenges.

When it comes to our resources, we're often driven by the notion that we don't have enough—this was the original temptation Adam and Eve encountered. Sometimes this is true; real financial challenges enter our lives. Often, however, this idea stems from the belief that *we* are not enough. We've listened to the serpents in our lives, those haunting thoughts and experiences that tell us something is missing, that we are missing out on life, and that God is insidiously at the center as the cause of this missed-out-on experience, whatever it is. Look at the story. By believing they lacked something, and by eating the forbidden fruit, Adam and Eve began to believe that intrinsically *they* lacked. So they hid from God and fought with each other. Our relationships to God, resources, and one another are so intertwined that when we experience pain in one area it makes an impact on all the others.

So we hide ourselves from God, and just as that primordial

couple hid in the garden's trees, we seek comfort by hiding behind our possessions. We hide the shameful parts of our lives from one another. We find in our hiding that we do not get what we seek, and over time we find ourselves disillusioned and hidden from even ourselves. In all our searching, we forget who we are, and so it's almost impossible to see others for who they are.

But God does not leave us there. He enters our story, engages us where we are, and leads us into the future of a renewed creation. We're active participants with God in this journey. He opens our eyes so we can see again, opens our hearts so we can feel again, and reminds us what it means to be human, again. God teaches us, through the Scriptures and by the Spirit, what it means to properly relate to resources, our money, and how to do so in a way that enriches our own lives and the lives of others.

As we grow in our awareness and maturity, we discover that more money is not what we're searching for, but that we're searching for God. Only when we realize a right relationship to money entails a right relationship to God, ourselves, and others can we experience the well-being for which we long. Money then becomes a tool to achieve our desires and do good in the world. Money, in the biblical tradition, is the raw material God uses to teach us to trust, to love, to serve one another, and to restore God's creation. God invites us to stand—with a God-centered perspective and life-style— as creative and loving alternatives to the prevailing culture, which centers on self and is ultimately based in fear. He also invites us to imagine what's possible. That, essentially, is a reclaiming of the very best of our religious memories, of Eden.

The way we handle resources is rooted in what we imagine is important, and what we imagine is possible. If misusing resources lies at the core of humanity's story of how we fell from Eden, perhaps one key to restore what has been lost is to use resources the way God has designed each of us to use them. And perhaps the way we handle resources is a signpost that points people back to what we all hope is possible, back to a loving life with a good and caring Creator, and toward loving-kindness with others. When each of us embraces our money types, collectively that signpost becomes even clearer, pointing people home.

What we've seen in this brief journey toward understanding our money types, however, is that God is enough. Because God is enough, and because we are made in his image, when our lives are attentive to God, we are enough; we are more than conquerors, and so whatever we have, whether much or little, does not define us. We define it.

We're called out into the open, out of hiding, and we can bring the ways we relate to money with us into the light. When we follow the lives of these seven biblical characters, we see that whether they were struggling through famine or reclining in luxury, God was at work in their lives, luring all things toward good. This is the story, both in joy and fear, in which we find ourselves. It's a story where the way we use money for good and for God has implications both now and into eternity.

Abraham types use money to demonstrate God's hospitable love.

Isaac types, with their disciplined maximization of resources, restore what is damaged, making all things new.

Jacob types call our attention to the truly beautiful and bring a taste of heaven to earth by using money in beautiful ways.

Joseph types connect us to what we need when we
> need it.

Moses types remind us that money can run our lives if
> we don't run our financial households decently and
> in order, putting God first.

Aaron types remind us of the sacrificial, others-centered
> love of God by the way they use money.

David types compel us, with hope, toward a better
> future, and call us to use our money toward noble
> purposes.

Together, these types provide an image of what is possible
when God is at work in our money.

Along the way to financial well-being, our eyes are dilating
and adjusting to new light; a fresh perspective develops as we see
money as a formative component in our spiritual growth. We're
beginning to see that more or less money does not mean more or
less happiness. We understand that God has uniquely designed us
to bring healing and restoration to the world through the way we
handle money. We're invited to trust—to trust that the way God
has made us is enough, and that while we always have room to
grow, we are affirmed by God and should therefore affirm others
in their growth into who God has designed them to be related to
money. We're called, together, to make the world beautiful, for it is
good. God affirmed it as such. And when we see goodness in our
relationships, work—and, yes, in our money—we have hope for
change, even in our homes, and perhaps in our own hearts.

Financial well-being is within your reach as you grow in your
money type. You can possess the confidence and insight necessary to handle money in a God-honoring way that's true to your

deepest sense of self and healthy in emotional, spiritual, and relational ways. Embrace your money type as a core component of your identity, as a sacred aspect of who you understand yourself to be—a God-imaged person who is God's partner in stewarding resources, loving others, and bringing hope into the world.

Prompts for Group Discussion

Discussing the topic of money types with other readers enriches your understanding and helps you embrace your own money type, while gaining a deeper appreciation for the joys and challenges faced by others. Use these prompts to generate dialogue.

- ✑ With which of the core characteristics or stories about your money type did you most resonate and why?
- ✑ Describe your earliest memory where you can see this money type in operation in your own life.
- ✑ What is the most challenging part about living with your money type?
- ✑ Given unlimited resources, what would money enable you to do?
- ✑ What is the prevailing or frequent thought or emotion you most regularly have about money? Do you wish this were different? If so, how?
- ✑ What do you wish people understood about the way you relate to money?
- ✑ "When it comes to money, it really annoys me when people . . ."
- ✑ How can others best support you in your relationship to money?
- ✑ Do you experience financial tension with certain people? If

so, in what way might your money type contribute to this tension?

- ✒ What is one thing you plan to do differently with money now that you understand your money type?
- ✒ Describe a time when you can clearly see your money type in operation.
- ✒ Describe a time when you can clearly see your shadow side influencing your financial thoughts, emotions, or actions.
- ✒ Can you think of the time when you felt most confident, secure, and at peace with money? Describe this situation.
- ✒ Have you ever felt as though God was at work through you by the way you used money? If so, describe this situation and the result.
- ✒ What is the greatest truth you've learned about your money type?
- ✒ With which money type do you experience the most tension, and why do you think this is so?
- ✒ Can you think of others in your life who might share your money type? When it comes to money, what do you most appreciate about them and what is most challenging about them?
- ✒ How do you see your money type evident in the character of God? For example, if your money type is Abraham (hospitality), how do you understand God to be hospitable?

NOTES

1. Leonard Fein, *Where Are We?: The Inner Life of America's Jews* (New York: Harper & Row, 1988), 198–99.

2. You may notice that all of the seven biblical characters are male. This is the Jewish tradition, and while recent attempts have been made to accompany each of the types with a female counterpart, for our purposes, and to remain true to the most original Jewish traditions, these additions, while helpful, are nonessential. Just as God's image is manifested in both men and women, the image of God revealed through each character's life transcends gender and is revealed in today's world by both men and women. In other words, just because the characters are male doesn't mean God's image is revealed as only masculine and that women should not read this book. The image of God revealed in each one is manifest and accessible by women and men. The lessons learned from each are not gender-biased or gender-specific.

3. All metaphors are inherently limited, and this is the case with *shadow* as well. It's important that we realize the concepts of light and darkness are being used to convey tensions in ways people intuitively can grasp, rather than to make value judgments about daytime and nighttime, actual light and shadows, dark colors or light colors—all of which are good and created by God.

4. While not everyone who would have visited Abraham could technically, under their customs and theological understandings, qualify as a stranger, A. E. Arterbury notes that, at its core, ancient Mediterranean hospitality involved supplying travelers with

protection and provision during their journeys. A. E. Arterbury, *Entertaining Angels: Early Christian Hospitality in Its Mediterranean Setting* (Sheffield, UK: Sheffield Phoenix Press, 2008). Amy Oden proposes that while those who were considered strangers in the Christian Testament differed greatly in what qualified them for such a title, one area of commonality is shared: "They are all vulnerable populations." Amy G. Oden, *And You Welcomed Me: A Sourcebook on Hospitality in Early Christianity* (Nashville: Abingdon Press, 2001), 19.

5. Greg McKeown, *Essentialism: The Disciplined Pursuit of Less* (Danvers, MA: Crown Business, 2015), 23.

6. Robert D. Lupton, *Toxic Charity: How Churches and Charities Hurt Those They Help (And How to Reverse It)* (San Francisco: HarperOne, 2011), 141–42.

7. This narrative presents obvious social and gender concerns for contemporary readers, particularly related to incest, polygamy, and objectification of women, which were not issues that concerned the original hearers of this narrative in the same way they do contemporary readers, but which deserve careful consideration today. Nevertheless, Jacob's love for Rachel is obvious, and is the focus of our attention at this time.

8. Leighton Ford, *The Attentive Life: Discerning God's Presence in All Things* (Downers Grove, IL: InterVarsity Press: Downers Grove, IL, 2008), 25.

9. Joshua Shmidman, "Jewish Beauty and the Beauty of Jewishness," retrieved online from Jewish Action, The Orthodox Union Press, http://ou.org.s3.amazonaws.com/publications/ja/5758/spring98/beauty.htm.

10. "Growing Good Corn," Inspiration Peak, http://www.inspirationpeak.com/cgi-bin/stories.cgi?record=142.

11. Henri J. M. Nouwen, *A Spirituality of Fundraising* (Nashville: Upper Room Books, 2010), 20.

12. It's interesting to note that Joseph informed Pharaoh that Pharaoh's two dreams were one and the same, and that because the dream

happened twice, it was fixed and God would bring it about. Joseph's dreams precede Pharaoh's dreams in the narrative. But by the same criteria Joseph applied to interpreting Pharaoh's dreams, we can infer that Joseph's dreams were one and the same, and that they were fixed and God would bring them about. Could this have given Joseph the confidence he needed to stay the course during all his impending mishaps?

13. Henri J. M. Nouwen, *Here and Now* (New York: The Crossroad Publishing Company, 1994), 25.

14. Merwin A. Hayes and Michael D. Comer, *Start with Humility: Lessons from America's Quiet CEOs on How to Build Trust and Inspire Followers* (Westfield, IN: Greenleaf Center for Servant Leadership, 2010), 5.

15. Walter Rauschenbusch, *Christianity and the Social Crisis* (London: MacMillan & Co., Ltd., 1920), 29.

16. Personal conversation with Rabbi Arthur Kurzweil in the fall of 2014.

17. Lister M. Matheson, *Icons of the Middle Ages: Rulers, Writers, Rebels, and Saints* (Santa Barbara, CA: Greenwood, 2012), 330.

18. While Flow Automotive's company practices are well known in the community, the distillation of these principles was recorded at the Global Leadership Summit in 2014. Copyright 2014 Willow Creek Association.

19. Henri J. M. Nouwen, *The Inner Voice of Love: A Journey through Anguish to Freedom* (New York, Image Books, 1999), 44.

20. Jean Vanier, *Becoming Human* (New York: Paulist Press, 2008), 88.